Pride Goes Before Destruction

Pride Goes Before Destruction

Human Vanity, Animal Agriculture, and
the New Covenant Solution

Matthew A. King

WIPF & STOCK · Eugene, Oregon

Wipf & Stock
An Imprint of Wipf and Stock Publishers
199 W. 8th Ave., Suite 3
Eugene, OR 97401

www.wipfandstock.com

PAPERBACK ISBN: 978-1-6667-4616-7
HARDCOVER ISBN: 978-1-6667-4617-4
EBOOK ISBN: 978-1-6667-4618-1

06/15/23

Dedicated to Ripley and Zira, for helping me to understand.

Contents

Acknowledgments

I WANTED TO FIRST thank Bible Hub for their tremendously helpful website, which allows for comparing the many biblical translations side-by-side.[1] Additionally, I want to acknowledge several individuals who assisted me in this work. Though I have never met them, I want to thank Martin V. Cisneros and James Bean for their exceptional scholarly work. I cite their work several times within this text. I also wanted to thank my brother-in-law, Samuel Cowley, who was enormously helpful in verifying the accuracy of the citations and references. Finally, I wanted to thank my wife, Nina, for always being supportive and encouraging despite this work taking many long hours of my attention.

1. biblehub.com

Introduction

IN MY EXPERIENCE, CHRISTIANS are overly hostile to animal rights. Any assertion that animals should be afforded equal, or even better, treatment than humans makes Christians uncomfortable. This discomfort is not based on logic, as we all commonly know that animals are like us in many ways. Humans and animals are both sentient, share the same types of organs and blood, and experience pain and suffering. Why are Christians so hostile to admitting that humans share a common experience with animals? That hostility can be explained with a frequently documented and discussed sin: pride. Human arrogance and vanity dominate Christian discussion about animals. This egotism is so ingrained in Christian culture that asserting the opposite is typically dismissed as being "Darwinian" or "anti-human."

This human vanity has caused the greatest atrocity we could fathom against animals. Annually, over seventy billion terrestrial animals are slaughtered for food around the world.[1] Most of these animals are shoved into close quarters, forced to lay in their excrement, and denied any ethical or compassionate concern. From birth to slaughter, the vast majority of animals endure an oppressive hell created by the worst of human behavior. This horrid situation would be a different story entirely if humans required the flesh of animals for health. Vegans and vegetarians are proof of the opposite. The vast majority of humans cause harm to animals merely out of habit, convenience, and taste pleasure, not because it is necessary. To complicate matters further, the atrocities we have committed against animals are causing massive destruction to ourselves. Hence the title of the book, which is derived from Prov 16:18. The verse states, "Pride goes before destruction, and a haughty spirit before a fall." Humans have shamelessly

1. Sanders, "Global Animal Slaughter."

destroyed planet earth and endangered our health due to our pride and vanity before other species. Fortunately, the Bible offers a solution.

This book could be seen as somewhat of a follow-up to my previous work *I Will Abolish the Bow: Christianity, Personhood, and the End of Animal Exploitation*. The main purpose of that book was to establish some of the tenets and principles that the Christian Animal Rights Association would administer in a quest to forge a more peaceful relationship between humans and animals. This book focuses on the human cost of the way we treat animals and also offers a biblically inspired solution. This text also addresses other biblical issues that affect animals that I did not include in *I Will Abolish the Bow*. In my previous work, I mostly took the Bible at face value. In this text, I am more concerned with alternative interpretations, the many different translations, and possible later additions regarding problematic portions of the Bible relating to animal rights. I also look at ancient extra-biblical texts that discuss early Christianity and its important figures. These works can support being merciful (Luke 6:36) to animals based on Judeo-Christian ethics. The first issue I want to address is human pride.

1

Human Pride

The Bible speaks resolutely against the sin of pride. Within this chapter, I am not talking about the word "pride" as it is used in our everyday vernacular to describe pride parades or "pride" related to being proud of something you accomplished. Instead, I am talking about the sin of pride. The word has many definitions depending on the context, but pride is best defined in this case as "an excessively high opinion of oneself; conceit."[1] Pride, in this instance, would be synonymous with hubris. The word hubris is best defined as "excessive pride or self-confidence; arrogance."[2]

The Bible criticizes hubristic pride several times:

> "Talk no more so very proudly, let not arrogance come from your mouth; for the LORD is a God of knowledge, and by him actions are weighed."
> —1 Sam 2:3

> "The fear of the LORD is hatred of evil. Pride and arrogance and the way of evil and perverted speech I hate."
> —Prov 8:13

> "When pride comes, then comes disgrace, but with the humble is wisdom."
> —Prov 11:2

1. "Pride."
2. "Hubris."

"Before destruction a man's heart is haughty, but humility comes before honor."
—Prov 18:12

"One's pride will bring him low, but he who is lowly in spirit will obtain honor."
—Prov 29:23

"But he gives more grace. Therefore it says, 'God opposes the proud but gives grace to the humble.'"
—Jas 4:6

I have always recognized this type of pride. I am part Italian, and that side of my family has always been incredibly prideful about their heritage. I will admit, Italian food is wonderful, but to that side of the family, everyone and everything from Italy is exceedingly glorified. From the food, the people, the culture, and everything in between—if it is from Italy, it is the best and nothing compares. Everybody that is Italian is to be trusted. Everyone from everywhere else is to be initially distrusted. Anything imported from Italy is the finest around. Everything imported from any other country is low quality. You get the point. Americans, too, have this excessive pride. Many Americans I know would proudly state, "The United States is the best country in the world." That would be fine if there were some objective standards they were consulting—for instance, if they said, "The United States is the best country in the world because studies show [fill in the blank]." Without standards or criteria, the statement that Italy or the United States is the best is just hubristic pride.

One of my favorite comedians is George Carlin. He was certainly no friend of Christianity, but he made a lot of great social critiques. Carlin humorously stated:

And I could never understand ethnic or national pride because, to me, pride should be reserved for something you achieve or attain on your own, not something that happens by accident of birth. Being Irish, being Irish isn't a skill. It's a fucking genetic accident. You wouldn't say, "I'm proud to be 5'11". [sic] "I'm proud to have a predisposition for colon cancer." So, why the fuck would you be proud to be Irish or proud to be Italian or American or anything? Hey, if you're happy with it, that's fine. Do that. Put that on your car. "Happy to be an American." Be happy. Don't be proud. Too much pride as it is. "Pride goeth before a fall." Never forget Proverbs, okay?[3]

That same idea of pride being reserved for achievement could be applied to race, sex, and even species. I never understood white supremacists who felt excessive pride about their skin color. I never understood misogynistic men who felt proud to be male. I never understood why we feel such excessive pride about our culture. As far as I can tell, none of us control into which body our consciousness is born. The same applies to our species membership. There is such excessive pride about being human when in reality, we could have easily been born into the consciousness of a cow, pig, or goat. I think collective humanity has an ego problem that is based on pride. Humans elevate themselves so far above animals. If you look at all forms of oppression and where they originate, it is usually based on pride. White folks thought they were more important than Black folks. Also, men thought they were more important than women. Indeed, many still feel that way, unfortunately. Thinking lesser of someone else allows one group to do whatever they want to another group without facing the moral repercussions of that behavior. Humans have done the same thing to animals. We portray them as lesser than ourselves because it reinforces our own ego and worth. I think that society continues to harm animals because it subconsciously elevates ourselves above them. It is based on hubris. I am not saying we have to go full Darwinian and believe we are just another animal. I am saying we share a lot in common with them, and what we share with them should be afforded equal consideration. Plus, our superiority over animals is not demonstrated when we behave just like them. For example, animals eat other animals and do not flinch. If humans were superior to animals, we would show kindness. Christians often worry that by elevating animals, we will lose our humanity; I would argue the opposite. By acting like animals (eating them, etc.), we prove that we are just another animal. Suppose humans were to demonstrate mercy towards animals and thus avoid killing them. In that case, I believe it would prove Darwin wrong—that we are not ultimately animals. This kindness and mercy would show that we are a different species. By showing true vegan dominion (Gen 1:26–29), we would then live up to our status as the *Imago Dei* (1:26–27), as it was intended in Eden (1:20—2:8).

Humanity, especially Christians, think that even their most trivial desires override the most essential needs of animals. Humans have made it

3. "George Carlin."

3

so that a momentary taste pleasure, like a sandwich, is far more important than the suffering an animal experiences for their entire short life. This pride has consequences. Human arrogance drives the destruction of animals and the destruction of our fellow humans. Our belief that humans are more important than animals is steadily driving us toward extinction and planetary destruction. Prophetically, our pride is killing ourselves. Proverbs 16:5 states, "Everyone who is arrogant in heart is an abomination to the LORD; be assured, he will not go unpunished." Proverbs 16:5 CEV states it like this: "The LORD doesn't like anyone who is conceited—you can be sure they will be punished." I truly believe the climate crisis, pandemics, and the widespread destruction of human health are God's punishment for human pride. Indeed, the title of this book is derived from Prov 16:18, which states, "Pride goes before destruction, and a haughty spirit before a fall." Unfortunately, Christians often have no idea of the link between animal agriculture and many of the world's problems. The next chapter takes a close look at the connection.

2

The Human Cost of Pride

CHRISTIANS OFTEN RATIONALIZE THE horrific crimes committed against animals with the justification that humans are "made in the image of God" (Gen 9:6). This reasoning has negative consequences for the animals. Additionally, this human arrogance is killing civilization with the results of modern animal agriculture. The days of Old MacDonald's farm are long gone. The vast majority of meat in the modern industrial world comes from "factory farms," which are synonymous with concentrated animal feeding operations (CAFOs).[1] Billions of animals are generally densely packed together, forced to lay into their feces and urine, and given antibiotics to prevent inevitable infections. Though the Bible is sometimes gruesome to animals, the confinement and intensive terror that humans put animals through in agriculture did not exist in biblical times. People in biblical times could probably not even picture such a nightmare. About 99 percent of farmed animals in the United States and more than 90 percent of global farmed animals exist on factory farms.[2] Thus, Christians who buy meat (and other animal products) from the vast majority of retailers are guilty of supporting animal cruelty, which is condemned in Prov 12:10 NLT. Animal products are terrible for the animals, but they have a high human cost. Humans threaten civilization with environmental destruction, climate change, infectious diseases, and antibiotic resistance. Animal agribusiness also heavily contributes to food poisoning, air pollution, and poor working conditions—all of which threaten human health and well-being. All of this

1. Loria, "What's a CAFO?"
2. Zampa, "99% of U.S. Farmed Animals."

horrible treatment of animals and sickening of ourselves would perhaps be justifiable if meat were undeniably necessary for human health and well-being. However, vegans and vegetarians are living proof that this is not the case. Humans can live perfectly fine and even thrive without the flesh of animals. Thus, how Christians interact with food is a biblical issue, including how it affects the environment.

Environmental Destruction

Many Christians I have met have a rather terrible view of environmentalism, usually borne out of hubristic pride and human deification. In the beginning, Adam was placed in the garden of Eden to keep and tend it (Gen 2:15). This verse means we have a significant role and duty in caring for creation. The Bible describes negative consequences when we fail to care for the earth (Isa 24:4–6; Rev 11:18). Importantly, humanity must remember that it is not our world to damage. Humans do not have an absolute say over what to do with the land God has given us. It is clear that God (John 10:30) made the earth (Neh 9:6; John 1:3 NLT) for himself (Col 1:15–16). God owns the land (Lev 25:23) and all of the earth (Exod 19:5; Ps 24:1), implying that it be treated with respect. Nothing about modern animal agriculture reflects the biblical understanding of how humanity should treat the environment.

For instance, animal agriculture requires substantial amounts of land to rear billions of animals. In fact, 45 percent of the earth's overall land is covered by livestock, and almost 50 percent of the conterminous United States is allocated to animal agriculture. Additionally, the leading cause of water pollution, habitat destruction, and species extinction is animal agriculture. Perhaps unsurprisingly, animal agriculture is culpable for as much as 91 percent of Amazon rainforest devastation. Habitat/rainforest destruction and species extinction are due to deforestation, which is driven by animal grazing and growing animal feed crops on converted land. Water pollution is caused by prevalent chemical fertilizers, pesticides, and herbicides utilized for livestock feed crop production, which end up toxifying rivers and streams. Another problem is fecal matter. In the United States alone, farmed animals produce nearly 3.5 trillion pounds of manure yearly.[3] Additionally, because of the manure produced by CAFOs, the air

---

3. "Facts," Cowspiracy.

becomes polluted with toxic gases like methane, hydrogen sulfide, and ammonia.[4] One study showed that those who live 1.5 miles from a CAFO are at a higher risk of reporting asthma and lung/nasal allergies than those who live 5 miles from a CAFO.[5] Supporting the products of factory farming is a failure of Christians to embrace Gen 2:15. Christians who support meat from CAFOs are guilty of the sins of polluting (Num 35:33) and defiling the land (35:34; Jer 2:7). On top of this, animal agriculture is contributing massively to climate change. Not only have Christians recklessly contributed to climate change, but they are also often quick to deny it outright. Regardless, farmed animals and their byproducts account for a minimum of 51 percent of global greenhouse gas releases.[6] Climate change causes five million worldwide deaths annually.[7]

Infectious Diseases

Animal agriculture is the root cause of many infectious diseases. Biblically, this should not surprise us. In *I Will Abolish the Bow*, I discussed the Tale of the Desert Quail (Num 11). In Num 11:4–6, the Israelites and others grumbled about the continuous manna God gave them (Exod 16:15), and they wanted other food to eat. So, begrudgingly (Num 11:18–20), God sent them quail. Importantly, those who consumed the quail flesh died from a God-sent plague (11:31–33 NLT), and their tombs were called the "graves of gluttony" (11:34 NLT). The Tale of the Desert Quail (Num 11) shows that meat can certainly lead to a plague.[8] Indeed, many recent infections show a similar pattern to the biblical example.

A human infection that originates from an animal is called a zoonosis. The United States Centers for Disease Control (CDC) states that 75 percent of novel or emerging infectious diseases are zoonotic. Throughout history, many of the most dangerous human infections arose from animal exploitation. For example, the Human Immunodeficiency Virus (HIV) is hypothesized to have been transmitted to humans by killing chimpanzees and monkeys for their flesh. Additionally, the Ebola virus might have been spread to humans by handling and killing bats for food. However, it is not

4. "Why Are CAFOs Bad?," para. 11.

5. Schultz et al., "Residential Proximity," para. 4.

6. "Facts," Cowspiracy.

7. Lombrana, "Climate Change."

8. King, *I Will Abolish the Bow*, 56–57.

just viruses. Infectious proteins dubbed "prions" cause "mad cow disease," which harbors in bovine flesh. Humans that eat this cow flesh can be infected with prions and develop variant Creutzfeldt–Jakob disease (vCJD). It does not end there. Many infections have arisen recently from animal agriculture.

Modern industrial agriculture is the root cause of many new and emerging infectious diseases. For instance, many Chinese meat markets sell live animals, which can spread viruses from animals to human shoppers or butchers. Most likely, the severe acute respiratory syndrome (SARS) virus, and possibly even the coronavirus disease of 2019 (COVID-19), emerged from these meat markets of China. This is not just a far-east problem, as influenza perpetuates because of factory farming. The virus transmits between chickens and pigs, rearranging its genetics and mutating. This is because of the horrible conditions seen on CAFOs, where animals are fed unnatural diets of corn and soy, crowded together, and are forced to lay in their own excrement. Those animals then inhale the toxic fumes from their urine and feces. These deplorable conditions make these animals more likely to become infected. Notably, the swine flu (H1N1), which caused a 2009 outbreak, is believed to have originated from a North Carolina pig farm.[9] Unfortunately, the 2009 H1N1 influenza caused as high as 575,400 global deaths.

Antibiotic Resistance

I was taught that resistance happens because patients do not finish their antibiotics as prescribed or doctors prescribe them inappropriately. However, this is probably not the primary resistance method, as close to 80 percent of United States antibiotics are used in agriculture. Animals are given antibiotics to prevent the inevitable infections they would acquire from their overcrowded conditions. This injudicious use of antibiotics contributes to the emergence and spread of resistant bacteria, such as methicillin-resistant *Staphylococcus aureus* (MRSA). These medication-resistant infections cause thirty-five thousand annual US deaths. When Christians pay for the vast majority of meat (and other animal products), they contribute to climate change, infectious diseases, and antibiotic resistance, which makes them guilty of indirect murder of their fellow humans. As we all know, the Bible condemns murder (Exod 20:13).

9. King, *Meat: The New Cigarette*, 31–33.

Food Poisoning

Meat is frequently recalled due to its contamination with infectious microbes. This contamination happens because when animals are slaughtered, the contents of their bowels often mix with the meat portions. In 2015, it was found that 24 percent of retail raw chicken in the United States harbored *Campylobacter*. Similarly, 1.5 percent of whole chickens at big plants in the US were found to harbor *salmonella*. Finally, morbid *Escherichia coli* (*E. coli*) infections are caused by factory farming. Cows are fed grain instead of grass, encouraging the growth of potentially disease-causing *E. coli*. Many citizens believe that these food-borne bacteria come from vegetables because items like romaine lettuce and leafy greens are often contaminated. However, the origin of these bacteria is from farmed animals. Outbreaks from leafy greens occur from fertilization by contaminated manure, tainted water irrigation, or the vegetables touching soiled flesh. Similarly, romaine lettuce outbreaks can arise from being irrigated with water that encountered a CAFO.[10] Not only does animal agriculture contribute to environmental destruction and infections, but it also wastes precious resources.

Wasting Resources

In John 6:11–12, Jesus told his disciples not to waste any food. Today's animal agriculture is responsible for 40 percent of total global harvested crop waste. Most crops fed to livestock are metabolized through the animals, which cannot be used for human nutrition. Worldwide, farmed animals eat five times the amount of food as all humans. Dairy and meat supply only 18 percent of human calories but use a whopping 83 percent of farmland. Despite all of this food production, one in nine humans goes to bed hungry.[11] Additionally, animal agriculture tremendously wastes water. Of all the water the United States consumes, 55 percent is from animal agriculture. Worldwide, animal agriculture consumes as much as 33 percent of total freshwater.[12] Hardly anyone in the modern world needs meat to live happily and healthily. Thus, this irresponsible waste of resources is a biblical issue. Christians who support animal agriculture violate Jesus' command

10. Morris, "From E. Coli to COVID-19."
11. "How Would a Vegan."
12. "Facts," Cowspiracy.

not to waste food. I apply the principle of John 6:11–12 broadly to all life-sustaining resources.

Chronic Diseases

Purchasing from the industrialized meat industry is harmful to communities and individuals due to their food choices. The Bible criticizes gluttony (Prov 23:2 NIV; Phil 3:19). One does not need to go far to see that the United States has a major obesity problem. The US is the world leader in obesity.[13] Research has revealed that meat consumption significantly contributes to global obesity. Furthermore, eating meat is linked with many other diseases and pathologies. For instance, processed and unprocessed red meat consumption is associated with hypertension. Frequent consumption of processed meat is associated with colorectal cancer. Although, a UK study discovered that even moderate consumption of red and processed meat increased the probability of developing intestinal malignancy. Expectedly, increased red meat ingestion (especially processed) is linked with an overall elevated mortality rate. Additionally, elevated ingestion of red meat and poultry is associated with an increased risk of developing diabetes. It is not just meat either, as dairy consumption is associated with cancers, such as female breast and male prostate. Finally, high egg consumption is linked to an increased probability of cardiovascular disease and mortality.[14] The individual does not just harm themselves when they eat meat, but also the workers who prepare the flesh.

Poor Working Conditions

No sane human being would want to work in a slaughterhouse. Humanity has a natural aversion to killing animals. Thus, the industry relies on exploiting workers who often have limited options. United States meat processing and abattoir employees are largely Brown and Black people who reside in underprivileged neighborhoods. African Americans have historically been a substantial percent of the staff, with more recent times seeing a flood of Latin American employees. Presently, about 38 percent of flesh processing and abattoir employees were not born in the United

13. King, *Meat: The New Cigarette*, 4.
14. King, *Meat: The New Cigarette*, 25–28.

States. Meat processing and slaughterhouse work is hazardous, as it combines sharp instruments in a congested and fast-paced setting. Thus, injuries are expected. Most abattoirs and flesh processing facilities run almost 24/7, and the speed at which animals are slaughtered and processed is barely regulated. The job entails repetitive movement and long hours, which leads to elevated injury risk. These employees experience chronic pain in their backs, shoulders, and upper extremities. An eight-hour stint is both cognitively and physically draining. In the flesh processing industry, injuries are often unreported due to the typical staff member's fear of losing their employment and various other reasons. Additionally, even though these hazardous circumstances exist, meat processing and abattoir employees receive a relatively small salary.[15]

Perhaps most significantly, the type of work that requires someone to shut off their natural sense of compassion towards animals carries with it a deadly toll for humans too. For instance, one study found that employment at a slaughterhouse increases arrests for rape and other sex offenses, violent crime, and total arrest rates compared to other industries.[16] Thus, to support the industrialized meat industry is to cause another to sin. Rape (Deut 22:25–27), violence (Prov 3:31), and law-breaking (Rom 13:1–3) are biblically condemned and thus sinful. Many Christians believe that causing others to sin is not a sin. However, on the contrary, Jesus stated to his disciples in Luke 17:1–2 (CEV), "There will always be something that causes people to sin. But anyone who causes them to sin is in for trouble. A person who causes even one of my little followers to sin would be better off thrown into the ocean with a heavy stone tied around their neck." Thus, supporting industrialized meat production makes others more likely to sin through rape (2 Sam 13:1–14), committing violence (Prov 13:2), and breaking the law (Titus 3:1).

As I have demonstrated, animal agriculture has a high human and animal cost of death and suffering, yet is very much an industry that Christians support. First Corinthians 3:16 states, "Do you not know that you are God's temple and that God's Spirit dwells in you?" When we serve meat to believers—which is the root of all of these diseases and negative conditions—or eat it ourselves, we are actually destroying God's temple. No wonder all of these problems have arisen, as 1 Cor 3:17 states, "If anyone destroys God's temple, God will destroy him. For God's temple

15. "Slaughterhouse Workers."
16. Fitzgerald et al., "Slaughterhouses and Increased Crime Rates," 158–84.

is holy, and you are that temple." Fortunately, there is a solution. With all of this perhaps newfound information, what can Christians do to divorce themselves from the destruction and death coming from the animal agriculture industry? The solution is called "the new covenant," which I discuss in the next chapter.

3

The Bible's Solution:
The New Covenant

IN JOHN 8:12, JESUS described himself as "the light of the world." Jesus told his disciples (Matt 5:1–2 NLT) that they also are "the light of the world" (5:14). Different interpretations exist about what the "light" means, but I have explained it by thinking about the "dark." The dark is associated with wickedness (Prov 4:19), hardness of heart (Eph 4:18), evil (Isa 5:20; John 3:19; Eph 6:12), badness (Matt 6:23; Luke 11:34), suffering (Isa 8:22), foolishness (Eccl 2:13 NLT; Rom 1:21), lawlessness (2 Cor 6:14), and the power of Satan (Acts 26:18). The contrast would be light, which is associated with righteousness (2 Cor 6:14), goodness (Isa 5:20; Matt 6:22 CEV; Luke 11:34 CEV), blamelessness, and innocence (Phil 2:15). Light is also associated with good works (Matt 5:16), truth (John 3:21), and wisdom (Eccl 2:13), as well as the glory (Isa 60:19; Rev 21:23), works (John 3:21), and power of God (Acts 26:18). Christians are called to be "the light of the world." I think that Jesus was stating that Christians are called to be the light that challenges the world's problems that stem from the darkness. As stated previously, darkness is associated with evil. God says in Prov 8:13 CEV, "If you respect the LORD, you will hate evil. I hate pride and conceit and deceitful lies." To be "the light of the world," Christians then must challenge the evils of pride and conceit. As demonstrated previously, humans have become incredibly hubristic and prideful towards other species. This wicked, possibly even Satanic hubris and arrogance have created much suffering towards animals, and the side-effects are spilling over into human affairs. Based on what we observe with the world's problems, this speciesist arrogance has planted Christians firmly in the dark. However, it is not too late to turn towards the light (Acts 26:18). We can start to turn back toward the light by remembering what humans share with animals.

What Humans Share with Animals

Humanity tends to believe that animals were created for the sole purpose of serving them. However, the Bible indicates that God created animals to enjoy their lives. For instance, Ps 104:25–26 says that God created Leviathan to play in the sea. Job 39:13 NASB indicates that ostriches flap their wings with joy. Additionally, Job 40:20 describes wild beasts playing in the mountains. These verses alone show that animals were not put here to be slaves and commodities of humanity; they are much more. In fact, animals know and understand God and even follow his commands. For instance, 1 Kgs 17:1–6 describes ravens bringing food to Elijah after they were instructed to by God. Animals also acknowledge their Creator (Job 12:7–9), and Isa 43:20 prophesies that various wild animals will honor God. A basic reading of any translation of the Bible tells us that animals are not objects, and we share similarities to them, even though we generally do not like to admit it. We should remember both human and animal lives depend on the hand of God (Job 12:9–10). Just like humans (36:31; Ps 146:7; Acts 14:17), animals rely on God for food (Pss 104:21, 24–28, 136:25, 145:15–16, 147:9). Additionally, humans and animals both praise God (150:6). Likewise, Ps 145:9 says that God shows mercy to all that is created. Although fish, great sea creatures, and birds were created on the fifth day (Gen 1:20–23), humans and terrestrial animals were created on the sixth day (1:24–31). Just like humans build houses (Deut 8:12), birds build nests (Ps 104:17). Finally, just like humans live in houses (Hag 1:4), so too do storks live in fir trees (Ps 104:17), wild goats live in mountains, and badgers live in rocks (104:18).

Christians often do not know they have a significant theological link with animals. As stated in *I Will Abolish the Bow*, humans (Gen 2:7) and animals (1:20, 21, 24, 30, 2:19) are both made *nephesh chayyah* in the original Hebrew.[1] In Gen 2:7, the New Living Translation (NLT), and recently the New American Standard Bible (NASB) both declare that Adam came to be a "living person," which is repeated in 1 Cor 15:45 NLT and NASB. The NASB is widely considered to be the most accurate English Bible translation. In the NLT and NASB of Gen 2:7, the English word "person" translates

---

1. King, *I Will Abolish the Bow*, 12.

from the Hebrew *nephesh*. This Hebrew word also describes animals in Gen 1:20, 21, 24, 30, and 2:19. Yet, the NLT and NASB do not translate *nephesh* to "person" when describing the animals as they do with the human (2:7). In *I Will Abolish the Bow*, I discussed how animals (and humans) possessing *nephesh chayyah* should be a personhood recognition. Thus, animals should have legal personhood.[2] Despite humans sharing *nephesh chayyah* with the animals, humans are incredibly vain and prideful towards them. This conceit may help explain why *nephesh* is translated differently between humans and animals.

Additionally, the New Testament sheds some light on *nephesh*. Almost the whole original Old Testament was written in Hebrew, and the original New Testament was written entirely in Greek. Small portions of the Old Testament were written in Aramaic, most significantly in the books of Daniel and Ezra. Importantly, when the Greek New Testament translated the mostly Hebrew Old Testament, sometimes there was no exact word that matched. For instance, 1 Cor 15:45 NASB partially references Gen 2:7 NASB. To translate Gen 2:7's Hebrew term *nephesh*, Paul and Sosthenes (1 Cor 1:1) used the Greek word *psychēn* in 1 Cor 15:45. The NLT, NASB, CEV, and NET translations of 1 Cor 15:45 use the English word "person" to translate *psychēn*. Elsewhere, this Greek word is sometimes rendered as "soul" (Matt 16:26; Mark 8:36). The "soul" in Matt 16:26 and Mark 8:36 seem to describe a human's immortal essence. Additionally, *psychēn* translated through Google Translate renders the word in English as "soul." Since humans and animals share a *nephesh*, they seem to share a *psychēn* as well, since *psychēn* is considered a biblically equivalent translation of *nephesh*. Thus, *psychēn* may indicate that animals have immortal souls, just like humans do (Dan 12:2). Another possibility is that 1 Cor 15:45 BLB, KJB, ASV, ABPE, DRB, NHEB, and WEB sees Paul and Sosthenes (1 Cor 1:1) using the word "soul" (*psychēn*) in a different understanding. In the aviation or maritime sense, pilots and captains will sometimes say how many "souls" are on board an aircraft or ship, respectively. "Soul" in the aeronautical or nautical definition means "person." Additionally, *psychēn* has the root word of "psych," which forms many words in English—most notably the medical prefix for "mind." For instance, psychology is the study of the mind, and psychedelic is a mind-expanding drug. These possibilities make it sort of unclear what Paul and Sosthenes (1:1) were trying to say in 1 Cor 15:45. Most clearly, I think *psychēn* (15:45 NLT/NASB/CEV/NET) further

2. King, *I Will Abolish the Bow*, 11–13.

supports that *nephesh* should be understood as "person" for animals like it is with humans (Gen 2:7 NLT/NASB). Furthermore, I explained in *I Will Abolish the Bow* that animals and humans have spirits (Eccl 3:21) that are implied to be eternal (12:7). Spirits and souls are suggested to be joined but divisible (Heb 4:12).[3] Thus, the word *psychēn* and its relationship to *nephesh* may also confirm that animals have immortal souls, which would be attached to their spirits (4:12).

There are more similarities. For instance, humans and animals are both described as the Hebrew *'am*. When describing a group of humans in the Old Testament, this Hebrew word is often translated to English as "a people" (Num 22:5; Deut 33:29; Jer 50:41; Ezek 3:5). Remarkably, animals are also described with the same Hebrew term. For instance, ants (Prov 30:25) and rock badgers (30:26) are described as *'am*, which are both also translated to English as "a people." Furthermore, humans and animals have a common origin. God created Adam from "dust from the ground" in Gen 2:7. Explicitly, the Lord formed every wild animal and flying bird from "out of the ground" in Gen 2:19. Implicitly, God made all terrestrial animals from the ground (1:24–25). However, Eccl 3:20 expands on this, stating humans and animals (3:18–19) "all go to one place. All are from the dust, and to dust all return." The Bible shows that humans share these many important characteristics with animals, which should be enough for humans to stop being so vain and arrogant about their species membership. There remains one theological hurdle, however.

Most Christians know they are "made in the image of God" (Gen 1:26–27). In Eden (2:15), being "made in God's image" (1:26–27) meant humans had responsibility (1:28).[4] Additionally, in Eden (2:8), based on *nephesh chayyah*, humans and animals were implied to be of equal intrinsic value. It was not until Gen 9:3–6, after the fall (3:1–6), that human life was implied to be more important than animal life because of being "created in the image of God." Jesus implied (Matt 6:26, 12:12; Luke 12:24) and directly stated (Matt 10:31; Luke 12:7) that humans are more valuable than animals. Jesus may have been referencing Gen 9:3–6. However, Jesus also encouraged believers to work toward the ideals of Eden (Matt 19:1–9).[5] Thus, I think Jesus meant that ideally, humans have greater value than animals because of physical attributes. Humans can serve animals (Mark 9:35)

3. King, *I Will Abolish the Bow*, 79–80.
4. King, *I Will Abolish the Bow*, 20.
5. Keener, "Jesus Summons Us."

like a good king (Ps 72:1–17). The king is not intrinsically more valuable than the citizens, just more valuable because of their leadership. Similarly, humans, who are made in God's image (Gen 1:26–27), are more valuable than animals because of their ability to lead (1:28).[6] Indeed, in Eden (2:15), humans showed servant leadership (Luke 22:25–26) over the animals (Gen 1:26–28). Later, Noah showed servant leadership by building the ark and rounding up a female and male of every animal type to bring aboard and preserve their lives (6:14–22). Similarly, Isa 11:6 prophecied peaceful human leadership over animals on the eternal new earth (65:17–18). Isaiah 11:6 states, "The wolf shall dwell with the lamb, and the leopard shall lie down with the young goat, and the calf and the lion and the fattened calf together; and a little child shall lead them." If Jesus was saying that humans are more valuable than animals (Matt 6:26, 10:31, 12:12; Luke 12:7, 12:24) based on the fallen conditions of Gen 9:3–6, it appears that humans and animals were still considered intrinsically equal on this fallen cursed earth (3:17–19). This intrinsic equality can be seen with the concept of biblical animal sacrifice (Lev 4:1—5:19).

Animal Sacrifice Shows Human and Animal Equality

Animals would have to be equal to humans for the sacrifice of Christ (1 Cor 5:7) to make any sense. Animals were sacrificed in the Old Testament (Lev 4:32–35) as a temporary (Heb 10:4) atonement (Exod 29:36)/forgiveness of sin (Heb 9:22), with Jesus being the ultimate and final sacrifice (10:1–18). Animal sacrifice reveals the seriousness of sin. According to the penal substitution theory of the atonement, God punishes humans who sin with death (Gen 2:16–17; Ezek 18:3–4; Rom 6:23). In order to forgive human sin, bloodshed (death) is required (Heb 9:22). Leviticus 17:11 says that blood makes atonement, meaning the demise of an animal. The earliest this happened was back in Gen 3:21 when God seemingly killed an animal (perhaps multiple) to temporarily (Heb 10:11 NLT) atone (Lev 17:11) for Adam and Eve's sin (Gen 3:6). The seriousness of sin was frequently made clear in the Bible as the human who sinned was required to die (Rom 6:23). Instead, an unblemished (flawless) animal was sacrificed and considered an acceptable, and theoretically equal, substitution. The animal took the penalty that was deserved for the human's transgression. Thus, the human was temporarily (Heb 10:4) forgiven their sin (Lev 4:27–35 GNT). Importantly,

6. King, *I Will Abolish the Bow*, 74–76.

Christ, also unblemished and flawless (1 Pet 1:19 GNT), was sacrificed (Heb 10:12) as a substitute in place of ungodly sinners (Rom 5:6–8).

One notorious story of animal sacrifice that begs for discussion occurs in Gen 4:1–8. God was pleased with Abel's animal sacrifice (4:4 CEV) over Cain's offering of fruit (4:3). God may have found favor in Abel's sacrifice because of quality, not substance. Genesis 4:2 says that Abel was a shepherd and Cain was a farmer. Abel brought the firstborn of his herd (4:4), while Cain just brought some seemingly regular old fruit as an offering (4:3). "Firstborn" implies importance and significance. Thus, maybe God liked Abel's animal sacrifice better because they were the firstborn. God later showed particular interest in the firstborn of any species, human or animal of Israel (Exod 13:2; Num 3:13; 8:17). God loved Israel (Hos 11:1), symbolically calling the nation his firstborn son (Exod 4:22). The equality of humans and animals is on display later, as God was pleased (Isa 53:10 HCSB; Matt 17:5) with the sacrifice of his firstborn son (Heb 1:6 CEV), Jesus (10:8–14). This situation is like earlier, when God was pleased with Abel's firstborn lamb sacrifice (Gen 4:4 CEV). Fittingly, Jesus is known as the "Lamb of God" (John 1:29). We seemingly have a bit of a contradiction, though. Genesis 4:4 CEV indicates that God was pleased with Abel and his sacrifice. However, Heb 10:6 CEV states, "No, you are not pleased with animal sacrifices and offerings for sin." This contradiction can be resolved when we consider that God is pleased with the sacrifice, depending on the condition of the offeror's heart. The sacrifices functioned as a ritual illustration of what God desired (Deut 10:12 CEV), which is to love him (6:4–5). Importantly, Hos 6:6 CEV states that God desires faithfulness and knowledge of him rather than offering sacrifices. However, the Israelites worshiped idols while still offering sacrifices to God. They were doing the ritual, but it meant nothing because they were not faithful to God or knowing (Hos 6:6 CEV) and loving him (Deut 6:4–5). Analogously, it would be like someone going to church but not listening or paying attention to the music or sermon. The sacrifices became an empty tradition rather than an expression of love for God.[7] With this understanding in mind, Heb 11:4 clarifies that Abel offered a better sacrifice than Cain *by faith*. Hebrews 11:6 then implies that faith was what pleased God. Meanwhile, 1 John 3:12 states that Abel behaved righteously and associates Cain with evil. This declaration makes sense, as Cain killed Abel (Gen 4:8). Therefore, God was pleased with Abel because his sacrifice was an expression of faith. Why, then, was

7. Houdmann, "Why Does God Desire Mercy."

God pleased (John 8:29) with the sacrifice of Jesus (1 John 2:1-2 NLT)? It seems to be because Jesus went forth with God's will (Heb 10:8-10).

Another well-known animal sacrifice occurs in Gen 22:1-14, which is known as the Binding of Isaac. In Gen 22:1-2, God tells Abraham to sacrifice his beloved son Isaac as a burnt offering. In Gen 22:9-12, Abraham bound Isaac and was ready to kill him before an angel stopped the father. In Gen 22:13, Abraham sacrificed a nearby ram as a burnt offering instead. The story demonstrates Abraham's faith in God (22:8; Heb 11:17) even in the worst scenarios. However, the Binding of Isaac (Gen 22:1-14) also seems to show that humans and animals are inherently equal, as the ram was considered a worthy sacrificial substitute for Abraham's son (22:13). This story was also a foreshadowing of Jesus, who sacrificed himself (Eph 5:2) in place of ungodly sinners (Rom 5:6-8).

Leviticus 6-7 talks extensively about animal sacrifice. Leviticus 6:1-5 discusses the seriousness of sin, committing sins, and their restitution. Leviticus 6:6-7 states that God (6:1) wanted an unblemished ram (or a comparable animal) as a guilt offering and that forgiveness with atonement will come with the sacrifice. Similarly, Lev 7:1-5 gruesomely describes the process of the animal sacrifice for the guilt offering, and 7:13-15 outlines the process for a sacrificed animal for the peace offerings. Leviticus 7:36 declares these animal sacrifices as a permanent law. Notably, the flesh of the animal sacrifices was required to be eaten by the priest (6:25-26, 7:7, 7:14-15) or allowed to be consumed by the priest's male family (6:29 NLT, 7:6 NLT). The priest could also have the offered animal's hide (7:8 NLT). As I discussed in *I Will Abolish the Bow*, Jesus displayed equality with animals by taking their place as a sacrifice instead (1 Cor 5:7), which eternally stopped animal sacrifices (Heb 10:15-18).[8] Jesus ended the sacrificial system of Lev 6 and 7 and the Passover lamb sacrifice requirement (Exod 12:1-28). Jesus ended the sacrifice of animals and the eating of meat in these situations. The Passover was replaced with the Lord's Supper (Luke 22:17-20),[9] and the animal sacrifices (Lev 6-7) were replaced with Jesus' sacrifice (Eph 5:2). Even the sacrificial system meat-eating was replaced symbolically, as Jesus stated to eat his flesh (John 6:53-54) instead. This equality with animals is signified in the Bible's declaration of Jesus as the "Lamb of God" (1:29).

Although, Heb 9:23-24 implies that Jesus is a better sacrifice than animals. Jesus' sacrifice (7:27 CEV) appears to be better because it ended the

---

8. King, *I Will Abolish the Bow*, 72-73.
9. King, *I Will Abolish the Bow*, 81.

sacrificial system forever (9:26, 10:15–18), which animal sacrifices could not do (10:4) and thus had to be repeated daily (10:11). However, we must remember that although Jesus is human (John 1:14), he is also God (Titus 2:13) and one with the Father (John 10:30). Job 33:12 proclaims that God is superior to any human. Although, the location may also help explain why Jesus was a better sacrifice. Hebrews 9:23 NLT states that the earthly tabernacle (Num 3:7 NLT) was a copy of the tabernacle in heaven (Heb 8:5 NLT). The earthly tabernacle required the blood of sacrificed animals to be purified. However, the real tabernacle in heaven had to be purified with a better sacrifice (9:23 NLT), specifically the blood of Christ (9:11–12 NLT). Thus, because the heavenly tabernacle is greater than the earthly Tabernacle (9:11 NLT), it needed a corresponding greater sacrifice (9:23 NLT). Regardless, Jesus is God (John 20:26–28). Thus, I do not think "Jesus as a greater sacrifice" negates the premise that animal sacrifices show us the intrinsic equality between humans and animals, because again, God is greater than any human (Job 33:12). Furthermore, Eccl 3:18 CEV confirms this premise of equality, stating, "I know God is testing us to show us that we are merely animals." Although, in context, this may only be regarding death and the afterlife (3:19–21 CEV). In conclusion, biblical commentator Martin V. Cisneros summarizes this equality well, stating, "Ecclesiastes chapter 3:19–21 says that animals are equal with humans. Otherwise, how could they have atoned for man, for a season (until Jesus came, who's blood is superior in TOTALLY redeeming animal, man, and angel) in the Old Testament blood sacrifices."[10] Notwithstanding, our Lord showed equality with animals in other ways throughout his ministry.

Jesus' Ministry Showed Concern for Animals

Significant moments in Jesus' ministry were conducted alongside animals. For instance, Jesus was born in Bethlehem. Mary gave birth to him and rested him in a manger, which is a feeding trough for livestock animals (usually). The text does not say it specifically, but Jesus may have been born (Luke 2:4–7) humbly alongside the animals. This beautiful scene is often depicted every year in ever more elaborate nativity scenes across the world. My favorite depiction of Jesus' birth amongst the animals was in the animated film, *The Star* (2017). The film depicts a donkey, dove, sheep, and a variety of other (mostly) domesticated animals who become witnesses to

10. Cisneros, "Hosea 2:18," para. 26.

the nativity of Jesus.[11] Similarly, Matt 4:1–11, Mark 1:12–13, and Luke 4:1–13 describe the temptation of Jesus in the wilderness by Satan. Mark 1:13 makes an explicit point of mentioning that Jesus (1:9) was with the wild animals. I found it odd at first that this was mentioned. There is nothing clear as to why, but the only logical conclusion I could deduce is that Mark 1:13 was probably trying to say that Jesus found comfort amongst them. Perhaps Jesus enjoyed their company as friends? Mark 1:13 also mentions that Jesus (1:9) was being ministered by the angels, which probably means that the angels were taking care of him. Perhaps Jesus was being taken care of by the animals too!

Animals Sometimes Outshine Humans

Animals may have spiritual insight far greater than we can understand. For instance, you may be familiar with the story of Balaam and his unnamed donkey in Num 22:1–41 CEV. On orders from King Balak (22:10–11 CEV), Balaam rode his donkey to Moab (22:21–22 CEV) to curse the Israelites (22:4–6 CEV). God did not want the Israelites cursed (22:12 CEV), and God became angry at Balaam for going. Thus, an angel of the Lord got in Balaam's way on the road to Moab. Surprisingly, the donkey Balaam was riding (22:22 CEV) saw the angel of the Lord (22:23 CEV). It was not until God gave him the ability that Balaam could see the angel too. The text does not indicate that the donkey required divine assistance to see the angel, unlike Balaam, who did (22:31 CEV). Thus, animals may have spiritual insight that humans are not gifted. This account reminds me of the movie *Ghost* (1990), even though the film does not exactly portray a biblical worldview. Regardless, Patrick Swayze plays a murdered banker named Sam Wheat. He stays around as a ghost to protect his girlfriend, Molly (Demi Moore), from the greedy man who (accidentally) had him killed. Sam's apparition form is ordinarily unperceived by most of humanity, except for psychic Oda Mae Brown (Whoopi Goldberg). Although, Molly's cat, named Floyd, can also sense Sam's ghost.[12] Just like this fictional story, in reality, animals may be more tuned into spiritual happenings than we humans are, as the unnamed donkey demonstrated.

It is also important to remember that humanity is ultimately responsible for all of the tragedies in the world. It was not animals that brought

11. Reckart, *The Star.*
12. Zucker, *Ghost.*

sin into the world—it was humans. As I explained in *I Will Abolish the Bow*, humans and animals were created to be friends (Gen 2:19–20) in Eden.[13] In the garden of Eden (2:15), humans and animals were to live harmoniously, peacefully, and only eat plants (1:20–30). God called this peaceful vegan paradise "very good" (1:31). Implicitly, in Eden (2:15), humans and animals were to live eternally with good health. However, Adam and Eve disobeyed (3:1–6) God (2:16–17) and brought sin into the world, although only Adam was held responsible (Rom 5:12 NLT; 1 Cor 15:22). This disobedient "fall" (Gen 3:1–6) brought death (3:19) and disease (3:16) for humanity and animals (Rom 8:20–23 CEV). Romans 5:12 CEV confirms this, stating, "Adam sinned, and that sin brought death into the world. Now everyone has sinned, and so everyone must die." Animals then suffered because of human action, much like animals suffer at the hands of humans today. Adam expelled them from paradise (Gen 1:20–31) and brought them into a hellish world (Rom 8:20–23 CEV), which we perpetuate today with our endless torment of animals. Importantly, it was not animals that caused the fall; it was humanity (Gen 3:1–6). Eve was deceived (2 Cor 11:3; 1 Tim 2:14) by Satan (Rev 12:9), and Adam was allured by his evil desires (Jas 1:13–15 HCSB). Animals seemed to have been content in Eden (Gen 2:8), unlike the humans. Humanity, meanwhile, frequently discounts and even forgets the importance of Eden (2:15).

Longing for Eden

From a Christian perspective, one aspect that believers do not typically consider is the importance of Eden (Gen 2:8). In my experience, most Christians are not aware of how centrally important Eden (2:15) is in reading the Bible. This place is so significant that the ongoing theme in the Bible is that the entire cursed world (3:16–19) will be restored (Ezek 36:35) to the goodness seen in Eden (Gen 1:20—2:8). Again, the garden of Eden (2:15) was the place where humans and animals lived in harmony, with no harm or death (1:20–31). After Jesus returns (Matt 24:44), this cursed world will be like Eden again (Isa 51:3), and humans and animals will live in harmony and peace once more (Hos 2:18 NIV). For all eternity (1 Cor 15:42 CEV), humans and animals will be free from harm and death (Isa 11:6–9) on the new earth (66:22). People who lived in biblical times understood the significance of Eden (Gen 2:8). Modern Christians have generally lost

13. King, *I Will Abolish the Bow*, 30.

sight of this—most likely because of the secular understanding that it was a fictional place and a creation myth. However, if Christians focus with just a biblical lens, Eden (2:15) is incredibly important. Christians are supposed to keep Eden (2:8) in mind when we read the Bible and live our lives. This notion can be found in the Bible. For instance, Ezek 28:13 describes onyx stone being in the garden of Eden. Exodus 28:9–12 commands the high priest to wear onyx stones on the shoulder-pieces of their garment for remembrance. Additionally, onyx stones were required on the chest piece (28:15–20). The significance of this cannot be downplayed. Randy Alcorn in *Heaven* reasons that the shoulder onyx stones were to remind the Israelites of Eden.[14] I believe then that the ancient Israelites were to constantly think about Eden (Gen 1:20—2:8) and how it will one day be restored (Ezek 36:35). This is a far cry from Christians today, who often seem happy that humanity now has to reside in a fallen cursed world (Gen 3:16–19). Not that most believers are happy with death and disease for them and their family members; rather, because of the fall (3:1–6), Christians now get to eat their favorite treats of bacon, sausage, and steak. Instead of looking at these animal products as a result of the fall (3:1–21), churches instead widely embrace them.

A proper Christian understanding of these treats would be to view them as the ancient Israelites probably did—the result of a broken and dysfunctional world. Being happy with animal products is like being glad that death and disease (3:16–19) exist. These terrible facts of life result from the fall (3:1–6) and thus should not be invited into the church and praised. Christians need to reevaluate how they look at their favorite treats. Instead, Christians should be *longing for Eden*, not thankful it is gone. In fact, on the new earth (Rev 21:1), specifically the new Jerusalem (21:2), the city's wall foundations will be adorned with onyx (21:19–20). The presence of the onyx implies that the new earth (21:1) will be a restored Eden (Isa 51:3), although better.[15] The ancient Israelites were reminded of Eden (Ezek 28:13) with the onyx stones (Exod 28:9–12). Christians should also remind themselves of Eden (Gen 2:8) and be looking forward to the much better and perfect (Rev 21:4) world to come (Luke 18:30 CEV). Christians should not be content with the death and suffering of this current cursed world (Gen 3:16–19). Indeed, 2 Pet 3:11–13 CEV implies that Christians should look forward to the new earth and speed up its arrival by honoring and serving

14. Alcorn, *Heaven*, 243.

15. Alcorn, *Heaven*, 244.

God. If Christians had this viewpoint, we would see animal products as disgusting and vile, a perversion of God's original design of harmony and peace between humans and animals (Gen 1:20–31) that will be restored (Isa 11:6–9) on the new earth (66:22). I believe God wants Christians to embrace this view, as depicted by the new covenant in the blood of Jesus (Luke 22:20).

The New Covenant

Jesus is the guarantor (Heb 7:22) and mediator of the new covenant (9:14–15), which superseded the old covenant (8:13). The old covenant involved Israel and its people, the Israelites, who were required to obey God's laws (Deut 27:1–26). The Israelites would be blessed if they obeyed God (28:1–14) and punished if they did not (28:15–68). Under this old covenant, animals had to be sacrificed to temporarily (Heb 10:4) atone for human sin (Lev 6:1–7). In contrast, the new covenant, which was prophesied by Jeremiah (31:31–34), now includes both Jews and gentiles (non-Jews) (Rom 11:11–24).[16] Furthermore, the new covenant involves Jesus. He fulfilled the law (Matt 5:17) and thus made us right with God through our faith in Christ (Rom 3:22 NLT), which grants us salvation (Eph 2:8) and eternal life (John 6:40). The sacrificial death of Jesus (Mark 15:37) atoned for all sin (1 John 2:1–2 NLT), which ended animal sacrifice forever (Heb 10:12–18). Significantly, God often makes covenants with his entire creation. For instance, in Gen 8:20—9:17, God made a covenant with humans and animals, promising never again to destroy them or the earth with a flood. In return, humans were to procreate, not eat bloody meat, and value human life above animal life (9:1–7). The meat (9:3–4) was to only be from sacrificed, clean animals (8:20). Covenants are essentially a promise. Importantly, Hos 2:18 (NIV) states, "In that day I will make a covenant for them with the beasts of the field, the birds in the sky and the creatures that move along the ground. Bow and sword and battle I will abolish from the land, so that all may lie down in safety." Hosea 2:18 describes a restoration of that "very good" (Gen 1:31) vegan world that God created at the beginning, where humans and animals lived in peace with no death or violence (1:20–30). The covenant of Hos 2:18 is a promise that humans and animals will again live in peace without brutality or killing. Job 5:22–23 (NIV, BSB, NKJV, CSB, HCSB, LSV, YLT) and Ezek 34:25–31 seem to describe the

16. Houdmann, "Old Covenant vs New Covenant."

same covenant, similarly promising that humans and animals will live in peace with no death or violence.

When did the Hos 2:18 covenant start? In *I Will Abolish the Bow*, I applied it solely to the future eternal state, the new earth (Isa 65:17).[17] However, it could be that the Hos 2:18 covenant started with the blood (Luke 22:20) and, thus, the death (23:46) of Jesus. Hosea 2:18 then will grow and grow in greater fulfillment until it is fully accomplished on the new earth (2 Pet 3:13). Thus, like a seed, Hos 2:18 would plant, start small, and then grow and grow until it is finally fulfilled in its entirety on the new earth (Rev 21:1). Notably, Jesus said during the Last Supper (Luke 22:20), "This cup that is poured out for you is the new covenant in my blood." Similarly, I believe the Gen 8:20—9:17 covenant began when Noah sacrificed animals (8:20). The animals' blood started that covenant. At the Last Supper (1 Cor 11:17–34), Jesus created a new covenant in his blood (Luke 22:20). Just like the covenant of Gen 8:20—9:17 started with the shedding of animal blood (8:20 CEV), the new covenant of Hos 2:18 may have begun with Jesus' blood (Mark 14:24). The Gen 8:20—9:17 covenant included all humans and animals. Similarly, I believe the new covenant in Christ's blood (Matt 26:28) also involved humans and all creatures, as evidenced by Hos 2:18 NIV. Martin V. Cisneros stated it this way: "I have quoted 4 of the leading translations on Hosea 2:18 because this is such a neglected truth that I wanted it to be clearly shown at the start that I'm not reading anything into this verse from a pet-translation, but that it is a clear statement of God's Holy Word that man and animal are to walk in the New Covenant of Jesus Christ together."[18]

Importantly, the Hos 2:18 covenant supersedes the Gen 8:20—9:17 covenant. The Gen 8:20—9:17 "everlasting" covenant was made null and void, as evidenced by Isa 24:5. The latter verse states, "The earth lies defiled under its inhabitants; for they have transgressed the laws, violated the statutes, broken the everlasting covenant." With the covenant of Gen 8:20—9:17 terminated (Isa 24:5), we no longer have to view humans as more important than animals (Gen 9:3–6). With the covenant of Gen 8:20—9:17 defunct (Isa 24:5), the Hos 2:18 covenant has taken effect in its place. The animals' fear and dread of humans (Gen 9:2) is replaced with the animals feeling safe (Hos 2:18 NIV).

17. King, *I Will Abolish the Bow*, 20–21.

18. Cisneros, "Hosea 2:18," para. 12.

This idea of the new covenant of Hos 2:18 seeding and then growing and growing to its ultimate fulfillment has biblical precedent. For instance, the Bible discusses the kingdom of God (Luke 14:15) and its interchangeable synonym, the kingdom of heaven (Matt 22:2). As I explained in *I Will Abolish the Bow*, these expressions can refer to the kingdom being spiritually present in the hearts of the faithful (Luke 17:21). They can also refer to the eternal new earth (2 Pet 1:11).[19] Based on Heb 2:8 NLT, the kingdom of God/heaven is commonly understood as "here/already, but not yet." This phrase is known as "inaugurated eschatology," which means that Jesus initiated the kingdom (Luke 17:21) with his death (Matt 27:50) and resurrection (Luke 23:42; Phil 3:9–10), but the kingdom is not yet complete. The kingdom will be fulfilled in its entirely (Ps 145:13) when Jesus returns (Matt 16:27) and completes his creation of the new earth (Isa 65:17). In the meantime, Jesus wants us to help create the kingdom of God (Matt 6:33). This notion lines up with what he wants us to pray in Matt 6:10: "Your kingdom come, your will be done, on earth as it is in heaven." Jesus wants us to help build his kingdom now. I believe that this "kingdom assistance" is the point of his Parable of the Mustard Seed in Matt 13:31–32; Mark 4:30–32; Luke 13:18–19, and his Parable of the Leaven in Matt 13:33 and Luke 13:20–21. These parables both teach that the kingdom of heaven/God will plant, start small, and then grow as time goes on. Although, there is some debate about when the kingdom began. One source cites the Catechism of the Catholic Church (CCC), whose statement aligns with my interpretation. The source states, "The Kingdom of God began with Christ's death and Resurrection and must be further extended by Christians until it has been brought into perfection by Christ at the end of time (CCC 782, 2816)."[20] Just like the kingdom of God/heaven began with Jesus' death and resurrection (Rom 8:34), so too did the new covenant of Hos 2:18 start with Jesus' death (John 19:30). Just like the kingdom of God/heaven is growing in greater fulfillment, so too is the new covenant of Hos 2:18.

Importantly, there are several lines of evidence that Hos 2:18 started with Jesus' blood (Mark 14:24) and thus death (Matt 27:50). I believe Hos 2:18 began with the blood of Jesus (Luke 22:20) based on the proximity of the text cited in New Testament epistles. For instance, within Rom 9:25, Paul (1:1) explicitly references some of the words of Hos 2:23. Additionally, within 2 Cor 11:2, Paul and Timothy (1:1) seem to reference the words (or

19. King, *I Will Abolish the Bow*, 80.
20. "Kingdom of God."

at least the idea) of Hos 2:19. Since Hos 2:19 and 2:23 began with these New Testament portions, would not Hos 2:18 as well, since this verse is in the same section as the other two? Admittedly, prophecies often kaleidoscope, meaning they jump between time periods with no precise measure of when they occur. I am stating, however, that the seed of Hos 2:18 was planted with Paul's reference to nearby verses. This seed of Hos 2:18 would then grow and grow through time until it is fulfilled in its entirety on the new earth (2 Pet 3:13). The new covenant of Hos 2:18, beginning with the blood of Christ (Matt 26:28), is also supported when Jesus said in Mark 16:15, "Go into all the world and proclaim the gospel to the whole creation." Some translations of Mark 16:15, such as the BSB, KJB, NKJV, DRB, NAB, and the NET, say to speak the gospel to all creatures. Obviously, this doesn't mean literally preaching to animals about the work of Jesus (John 3:16; 1 Tim 1:15). I think it means for believers to help bring the eschatological kingdom of God (Dan 7:27) to all creatures, as much as possible, before its completion. This eternal kingdom (Luke 1:33) involves peace (Isa 9:6–7) and righteousness (2 Pet 3:13) for all creatures (Isa 65:25). I believe the gospel in Mark 16:15 is not just referring to Jesus dying (Acts 2:23) to atone for sins (1 John 2:1–2 NLT). The gospel in Mark 16:15 is also about restoring all creation back to its original peace and harmony (Gen 1:20–31). This restoration mission of the gospel is confirmed in Rom 8:18–25 and Col 1:20–23. However, the authenticity of Mark 16:15 is questionable. One reliable source states that essentially all scholars think that Mark 16:9–20 is a later addition.[21] However, biblical scholar Dave Miller, PhD, argues quite convincingly about the authenticity of Mark 16:9–20, concluding, "The reader of the New Testament may be confidently assured that these verses are original—written by the Holy Spirit through the hand of Mark as part of his original gospel account."[22]

The Root of Jesse

Hosea 2:18 does not seem to be the only verse about animals on the new earth (2 Pet 3:13) that was seeded with Christ. Isaiah 11:6–9 speaks of the new earth (65:17), where humans and animals will no longer harm each other—a restoration of Eden (Gen 1:20—2:8). Isaiah 11:6–9 has obviously not yet reached its final fulfillment. Isaiah 11:10 states, "In that day the root

21. Smith, "Ending of Mark's Gospel."
22. Miller, "Is Mark 16:9–20 Inspired?," para. 53.

of Jesse, who shall stand as a signal for the peoples—of him shall the nations inquire, and his resting place shall be glorious." In Rom 15:12, Paul (1:1) specifically references and paraphrases the words of Isa 11:10 and implies that Jesus (Rom 15:8–9) is this "root of Jesse." However, Isa 11:10 has not yet reached its final fulfillment. Matt 25:31 records Jesus speaking about his second coming, stating, "When the Son of Man comes in his glory, and all the angels with him, then he will sit on his glorious throne." This verse matches Isa 11:10's description of Jesus' glorious resting place. Isaiah 11:10 then was seeded with the arrival of Jesus (Luke 2:25–32). Isaiah 11:10 will be fulfilled in its entirety on the new earth (Rev 21:1) after Jesus returns (Matt 16:27). The new covenant of Hos 2:18 was seeded with Hos 2:19 and 2:23 being referenced with 2 Cor 11:2 and Rom 9:25, respectively. Likewise, I believe the same is true for Isa 11:6–9. Again, prophecies often kaleidoscope, but I am stating that the seed of Isa 11:6–9 was planted with Paul's (Rom 1:1) reference (15:12) of Isa 11:10. I believe these prophetic passages about the new earth (65:17), Isa 11:6–9 and Hos 2:18, were seeded with Christ's ministry. Thus, Jesus expects believers to work toward fulfilling Isa 11:6–9 and Hos 2:18, growing them as much as we can (Matt 6:10). Jesus will fulfill them entirely on the new earth (2 Pet 3:13) after his second coming (Matt 16:27).

The Behavior of Early Christians

Perhaps there was an awareness that with the blood of Christ (26:28), Hos 2:18 was part of the new covenant. Although not in the Bible, some ancient documents (dated between the second and fourth centuries) indicate that the original twelve apostles (Matt 10:1–4), and another biblical figure, lived without harming animals. These individuals knew Jesus well. I am not saying that any of these upcoming documents are authoritative or God-inspired like the Bible (2 Tim 3:16–17), but they merely support my thesis. For example, John was one of the twelve original apostles (Matt 10:2). John was recorded to have never eaten meat, as Christian historian Eusebius (c. AD 260–339) claimed in *History of the Church II*. Paradoxically, John was implied to be a fisherman in Mark 1:19 before following (1:20) Jesus (1:17). Similarly, Matthew was one of the twelve original apostles and a tax collector (Matt 10:2–3) before following Jesus (9:9). In *The Instructor*, book 2, chapter 1, Clement of Alexandria (c. AD 150–c. 215), an early church father, claimed that Matthew shunned meat and ate nuts, vegetables, seeds, and hard-shelled fruits. Thomas, one of the original twelve apostles (10:2–3), famously doubted the resurrected Jesus until he saw and touched the Lord's crucifixion wounds (John 20:24–29). In chapter 20 of the *Acts of Thomas*, the apostle Thomas is also recorded as having abstained from meat consumption.[23] The *Acts of Thomas* is dated between the years AD 200 and 225.[24]

The *Clementine Homilies* are dated between AD 300 and 320,[25] while the *Recognitions of Clement* are dated between AD 320 and 380.[26] Another apostle of the original twelve was Peter (Matt 10:2). Peter is documented in the *Clementine Homilies* and the *Recognitions of Clement*, saying, "I live on olives and bread, to which I rarely only add vegetables." In the *Clementine Homilies*, Peter stated, "The unnatural eating of flesh meats is as polluting as the heathen worship of devils, with its sacrifices and its impure feasts, through participation in it a man becomes a fellow eater with devils." Ironically, Peter famously experienced the "Vision of the Sheet with Animals," which is described in Acts 10:9–16 and 11:4–10, in which he was told to "rise, kill, and eat" (10:13; 11:7). Peter's abstention from meat could explain why he responded in Acts 10:14, "By no means, Lord; for I have never eaten anything that is common or unclean." Peter stated (11:4) similarly in Acts 11:8. Acts 10:14 and 11:8 reference meat from unclean animals (Lev 11:1–47; Deut 14:1–21). Although, Peter was also a fisherman before he followed Jesus (Matt 4:18–20). Regardless, there is evidence that all the apostles may have abstained from meat. In *Demonstratio Evangelica* (Proof of the Gospels), Eusebius (c. AD 260–339) stated, "They [the Apostles] embraced and persevered in a strenuous and a laborious life, with fasting and abstinence from wine and meat." Additionally, James, the brother of Jesus, although not one of the original twelve, was also said to be an apostle (Gal 1:19). Remarkably, according to multiple sources, James was recorded as having abstained from consuming meat.[27]

Based on this extrabiblical literature, it appears that abstention from meat was widespread among the apostles. This abstention is surprising given how well-off they were after Jesus' ascension (Acts 1:9–11). Acts 4:33–37 states,

23. Bean, "Evidence That Jesus."
24. Kirby, "Acts of Thomas."
25. Kirby, "Pseudo-Clementine Homilies."
26. Kirby, "Pseudo-Clementine Recognitions."
27. Bean, "Evidence That Jesus."

And with great power the apostles were giving their testimony to the resurrection of the Lord Jesus, and great grace was upon them all. There was not a needy person among them, for as many as were owners of lands or houses sold them and brought the proceeds of what was sold and laid it at the apostles' feet, and it was distributed to each as any had need. Thus Joseph, who was also called by the apostles Barnabas (which means son of encouragement), a Levite, a native of Cyprus, sold a field that belonged to him and brought the money and laid it at the apostles' feet.

It seems the apostles could have chosen to indulge but instead elected to refrain from meat. Did they perhaps know that Hos 2:18 began with the new covenant in Christ's blood (Mark 14:24)? The new covenant of Hos 2:18 taking root this early with Christians makes sense, as Col 1:19–20 states that Jesus' (1:13) blood made peace and reconciliation between God and everything on earth and in heaven.

Additionally, several early Christian figures criticized meat-eating, perhaps acknowledging the new covenant of Hos 2:18. For instance, the early church father and bishop Saint Basil the Great (AD 329–379) stated, "The steam of meat meals darkens the spirit. One can hardly have virtue if one enjoys meat meals and feasts. In the earthly paradise [Eden], no one sacrificed animals, and no one ate meat." The early church father Saint Jerome (c. AD 342–420) may have most significantly understood Hos 2:18 began with the new covenant in Christ's blood (Luke 22:20). Saint Jerome stated, "The consumption of animal flesh was unknown up until the great flood. But since the great flood, we have had animal flesh stuffed into our mouths. Jesus, the Christ, who appeared when the time was fulfilled, again joined the end to the beginning, so that we are now no longer allowed to eat animal flesh."[28] In all likelihood, Saint Jerome was referencing the new earth (Isa 65:17–25) and Eden (Gen 1:20—2:8), two places where animals are not harmed, when he said, "joined the end to the beginning." Eden (2:15) occurred at the beginning of biblical history (1:1). The new earth (Rev 21:1) will come at the end of biblical history (22:1). Additionally, the garden of Eden was formed at the beginning of the Bible (Gen 2:8–10). Finally, the Bible ends with a remade paradisiacal garden (Rev 22:1–5) on the new earth (21:1).

Several prominent early church figures may have believed the new covenant of Hos 2:18 started with the blood of Christ (Matt 26:28), based

---

28. Bean, "Evidence That Jesus."

on their behavior. Based on his recently cited quote, its' perhaps not surprising that the early church father, Saint Basil the Great, was purportedly vegetarian. Additionally, some other early church fathers, including Tertullian (c. AD 155–c. 220), Saint Clement of Alexandria (c. AD 150–c. 215), and Saint John Chrysostom (c. AD 347–407), were reportedly vegetarians. Similarly, Origen of Alexandria (c. AD 185–c. 253), a debatable early church father, was ostensibly a vegetarian. Saint Clement of Alexandria stated on the subject, "If any righteous man does not burden his soul by the eating of flesh, he has the advantage of a rational motive." Saint John Chrysostom stated, "The saints are exceedingly loving and gentle to mankind, and even to brute beasts . . . Surely we ought to show them [animals] great kindness and gentleness for many reasons, but, above all, because they are of the same origin as ourselves."[29] Much later, Saint Francis of Assisi (c. AD 1181–1226) became known for his concern for animals. In fact, he is known as the "Patron Saint of Animals." Saint Francis of Assisi stated, "God requires that we assist the animals, when they need our help. Each being (human or creature) has the same right of protection."[30]

It is hard to say for sure, but early Christians may have understood the new covenant of Hos 2:18 and its beginning with the blood of Christ (Mark 14:24). Many somewhat modern Christians have carried on this tradition. For instance, John Wesley (AD 1703–1791), the founder of Methodism, was a vegetarian. Similarly, the Salvation Army founders, William (AD 1829–1912) and Catherine (AD 1829–1890) Booth, author Leo Tolstoy (AD 1828–1910), and Ellen G. White (AD 1827–1915), a cofounder of the Seventh-day Adventist Church, were all vegetarians. Finally, Reverend Fred Rogers (AD 1928–2003), an ordained Presbyterian clergyman, was also a vegetarian. He is known more famously as the host of the children's television show *Mister Rogers' Neighborhood*.[31] God allowed meat consumption (Gen 9:1–4) only after associating the human heart with evil intention (8:21). I believe that because the world is not following the guidelines of the Hos 2:18 new covenant and following our evil ambitions instead, humanity is seeing so many problems with animal cruelty, human health, the environment, and poor working conditions. Psalm 107:33–34 environmentally exemplifies this notion, stating, "He turns rivers into a desert, springs of water into thirsty ground, a fruitful land into a salty waste, because of the

29. "Famous Vegetarians."

30. Francis of Assisi, "God Requires."

31. "Famous Vegetarians."

evil of its inhabitants." The next chapter focuses on the new covenant of Hos 2:18 and its potential benefits in healing the world.

4

Healing Our World with the New Covenant

HOSEA 2:18 AND ISA 11:6–9, though they find their complete fulfillment on the new earth (Rev 21:1), were first seeded with Christ. Hosea 2:18 NIV and Isa 11:6–9 indicate that humans and animals will live in peace and harmony for all eternity (65:18). This peace and harmony would imply a vegan diet and a world devoid of grievous animal exploitation, as Hos 2:18 NIV indicates that animals will safely rest. Similarly, Isa 11:6–9 indicates that humans and animals will live peacefully. This new earth (65:17) veganism would make sense, as it was the diet God wanted for humans and animals in the "very good" world (Gen 1:26–31) of Eden (2:8). This vegan continuity makes sense because the new earth (Isa 65:17) is a restoration of Eden (51:3). Meat and other animal products require much harm and suffering for animals, which does not fit with the descriptions of Isa 11:6–9 and Hos 2:18 NIV. Since these recently mentioned verses were seeded with Christ, our ministry believes we are to try and work towards (Matt 6:10) that peaceful and harmonious (Isa 11:6–9) new earth (2 Pet 3:13) as much as we can before Jesus returns (Matt 24:30) to complete it in its entirety (Rev 21:1). Thus, the Christian Animal Rights Association advocates a vegan diet.

Throughout the remainder of the book, you will see the term "plant-based diet" (PBD). This term is frequently used interchangeably with vegetarianism and veganism. This subtle difference is related to the approach. Veganism excludes all animal products. Generally, vegans are concerned with animal rights, convinced that ideally, animals should not be used as resources for humans. Vegetarianism only avoids the products that require the death of animals, like gelatin and meat. However, vegetarianism permits animal products that do not inherently require killing, such as eggs and dairy. "Plant-based diets" also includes pescatarianism. Pescatarians are almost exactly like vegetarians. The only significant difference is that pescatarians eat seafood but still shun all other forms of meat. PBDs also include "flexitarianism," which is essentially equivalent to "reducetarianism." Flexitarians and reducetarians are typically aware of the harm that animal agriculture causes and thus seek to significantly decrease their ingestion of animal products but not eliminate them. Veganism, vegetarianism, pescatarianism, flexitarianism, and reducetarianism are all encompassed under the category of "plant-based diets." PBDs share a common thread in placing plants as the centerpiece of a meal with either a reduction or complete abstention from all or some types of flesh and other animal-derived foods. "Plant-based" is also used to make a distinction about motivation. Since vegans are typically motivated by animal rights, "plant-based" is often used to say that one avoids animal products, but likely more for environmental or health purposes.[1]

The reader may be wondering why the Christian Animal Rights Association advocates for veganism when many believers of the past were just vegetarian. Biblically, Gen 1:26–29 shows that the ideal for humanity is veganism, as God created only the plants for food. However, post-fall (3:6–24), veganism was probably not possible for most of humanity to obtain all necessary nutrients. For instance, even with modern veganism, I have encountered that it can be difficult at first to get vitamin B12, zinc, iron, and omega-3s. To obtain these four nutrients usually requires creative solutions that may include breakfast cereals, specialty products, or supplementation. The closer you get to biblical times, the more that people of the past did not have those options readily available. Thus, though vegetarianism does not reflect the ideal of Gen 1:26–29, we believe it still mostly aligns as it focuses on not harming animals for food. Traditionally, dairy and eggs usually did not require harming animals. However, today, the dairy and egg industries are tremendously cruel (Prov 12:10 NLT) and barely resemble anything close to how milk (27:27) and eggs (Deut 22:6–7) were obtained in biblical times. Thus, if a believer was a vegetarian, it may reflect a concern for animals. Therefore, their actions mostly align with the new covenant of Hos 2:18. With veganism being much simpler to accomplish than in the past, we encourage believers to work towards the vegan ideal seen in Gen 1:26–29

---

1. King, *Meat: The New Cigarette*, 45–46.

and the new covenant of Hos 2:18. Importantly, this vegan feature of the Hos 2:18 covenant can bring many benefits to animals.

Animal Benefits

The new covenant (1 Cor 11:25) is expanded on in Hos 2:18 NIV. The latter verse states, "In that day I will make a covenant for them with the beasts of the field, the birds in the sky and the creatures that move along the ground. Bow and sword and battle I will abolish from the land, so that all may lie down in safety." Thus, the new covenant of Hos 2:18, beginning with the blood of Jesus (Mark 14:24), marks a turn away from exploiting animals to letting them live in peace. The new covenant of Hos 2:18 started with Jesus' blood (Luke 22:20). It will be fulfilled in its entirety (Isa 11:6–9) after his return (Matt 16:27). Therefore, implementing the Hos 2:18 new covenant solution of a vegan diet would bring profound benefits to our animal friends. There is nothing natural about how animals breed when exploited by industry. Animals are brought into the world to keep up with consumer demand. Widespread veganism among Christians would spare billions of animals from needless and gratuitous suffering, as fewer animals would be brought into the world to keep up with consumer demand. Importantly, Christians can divorce themselves from an insanely cruel industry where animals are treated as nothing more than commodities. After all, Prov 12:10 NLT links animal cruelty with human wickedness. By implementing veganism, Christians can live by the new covenant's vision of peace for all sentient creation (Hos 2:18 NIV). The new covenant of Hos 2:18 would be beneficial for animals and our collective environment.

Environmental Benefits

Veganism has enormous resource-preserving benefits. For instance, parallel to a heavy meat-eater, a vegan uses 1/13 as much water and 1/18 of the land for sustenance. An individual can make much impact. For example, a vegan saves forty-five pounds of grain, eleven hundred gallons of water, and thirty square feet of forested land every day. This conservation of precious resources reflects Jesus' command to not waste food in John 6:11–12. I apply the principle of John 6:11–12 broadly to all life-sustaining resources. New covenant (Hos 2:18) veganism has the potential to save lives. For instance, as far as climate change: a vegan diet creates half as much carbon dioxide as a heavy meat diet.[2] If the entire world switched to a plant-based diet in place of dairy and meat by 2050, it could potentially save as many as eight million human lives and make a two-thirds decrease in greenhouse gas emissions. Tellingly, University of Oxford researchers found that abstaining from dairy and meat products can reduce a person's food carbon footprint by as much as 73 percent.[3] Refraining from eating animal products can allow Christians to practically divorce themselves from water pollution, species extinction, habitat destruction, and Amazon rainforest destruction. Farming plants for human consumption does not require livestock grazing or growing feed crops for animals, eliminating a Christian's contribution to deforestation. As plants do not produce feces, abstaining from animal products also eliminates a Christian's contribution to manure production. Instead of committing the sins of polluting (Num 35:33) and defiling the land (35:34; Jer 2:7), a Christian that incorporates the new covenant (Hos 2:18) solution of a vegan diet will help heal the land (2 Chr 7:14). The new covenant (Hos 2:18) solution of a vegan diet would tend the land responsibly, just like Adam was entrusted to do in the garden of Eden (Gen 2:15). This responsible tending can help save lives (Ezek 18:32). The new covenant of Hos 2:18 can help heal the environment, as well as ourselves.

Human Health Benefits

Veganism is frequently praised in the Bible. For instance, after God created the earth and its inhabitants (Gen 1:1–28), God told humans and animals to eat only plants (1:29–30). God called this vegan world "very good" (1:31). Additionally, veganism is praised with the eponymous prophet's diet in Dan 1:1–21. Veganism is commended again with Ps 104:14–15, which implies grass as food for farm animals, plants as man's food, and bread to strengthen the heart of man. Additionally, veganism is implied to be the eternal diet (Isa 11:6–9; 65:25) on the future new earth (66:22), a restoration (Ezek 36:35) of Eden (Gen 1:20—2:8). The Bible praises good health (3 John 1:2), and veganism—God's preferred diet (Gen 1:29–31)—has fittingly been shown to prevent and even reverse many chronic illnesses. It is important to note that this means whole food vegan diets, not processed and vegan junk foods. These unhealthy vegan foods may see different health results than what is presented further. Regardless, research on

2. "Facts," Cowspiracy.

3. "Foodprint," para. 5, 9.

vegan diets suggests that they can protect against malignancies, improve cardiac health, and decrease the risk of type 2 diabetes. Based on a 2017 review, consuming a vegan diet can reduce an individual's cancer risk by 15 percent. Additionally, a large study from 2019 associated a high consumption of plant-based foods combined with a decreased ingestion of animal foods with a reduced risk of mortality and cardiac disease in adults. Furthermore, vegans tend to have a lower body mass index (BMI) than those with different diets. Indeed, 2015 study researchers testified that vegan diets had greater effectiveness in weight loss and supplying macronutrients than pesco-vegetarian, semi-vegetarian, and omnivorous diets.[4] Based on a review of studies, a whole foods vegan diet appears to be safe for type II diabetics and as helpful, if not more, than a standard American Diabetes Association (ADA) diet. Additionally, the review notes that vegans have a decreased risk of diabetes type II compared to non-vegetarians.[5] Truly, this evidence can be substantiated by the claims of nutrition organizations. For instance, the United States Academy of Nutrition and Dietetics states that informed vegan diets are appropriate for all ages, healthy, adequately nutritious, and may treat and prevent particular diseases. The organization also states that vegans have a decreased risk of type II diabetes, hypertension, obesity, specific cancers, and coronary artery disease. Similarly, Dietitians of Canada states that an informed vegan diet is high in antioxidants, fiber, and vitamins and low in cholesterol and saturated fat, which helps defend against chronic illnesses. Additionally, the organization states that vegans have decreased rates of diabetes, particular cancers, and cardiac disease compared to non-vegans. They add that vegans have reduced blood pressures when compared to vegetarians and flesh-eaters and that vegans are less prone to being overweight.[6]

Commerce functions based on supply and demand. Less demand means fewer animals have to be brought into the world. As previously discussed, most antibiotics in the United States are used in agriculture. To control antibiotic resistance, Christians should employ the veganism seen in the new covenant of Hos 2:18. Collective individual shunning of animal products would cause fewer animals to be factory farmed and given antibiotics to avoid infections. Additionally, widespread veganism has the potential to restrain the infectious diseases that come with closely detaining

4. Smith, "What to Know."
5. "Type 2 Diabetes."
6. Peter, "Is Being Vegan Healthy?"

animals for food, as it would not require large-scale animal confinement. The ceasing of using animals for food would theoretically drastically limit the chance for a pathogen to jump the species barrier between humans and animals. Conversely, there is no proof that plant viruses cause sickness in humans or animals. Similarly, with food poisoning, many of these bacteria arise from the feces of farmed animals. In a world where animals are no longer farmed, these feces would not exist in their vast quantities. Therefore, the manure would be less likely to contaminate surrounding communities and food. Indeed, one study indicated that vegans and vegetarians are less probable to develop food poisoning than meat-eaters. Additionally, adopting a vegan diet can allow one to divorce themselves from the enormous quantities of manure that farmed animals create. Importantly, plants do not generate feces.[7] Thus, veganism can help spare fellow humans from the various health conditions tied to their residence near CAFOs. The new covenant of Hos 2:18 is beneficial for animals, the environment, and individual health and very helpful for the workers employed in the abattoirs.

Working Conditions

On the surface, the widespread implementation of the vegan new covenant solution of Hos 2:18 would put many workers out of a job. That is a common line of reasoning actually—that somehow meat-eaters are doing a favor to workers by keeping them employed. However, widespread adoption of veganism would allow those workers to transition to different jobs. These jobs would probably be far more peaceful, dignified, and wholesome. Importantly, Mercy for Animals and Miyoko's Creamery have announced programs to assist livestock farmers in transitioning away from that business.[8] Although, there lies a bit of hypocrisy regarding concern for these workers. For instance, modern society is generally appalled by slavery and slave-owners. Despite the Bible's tolerance of slavery (Eph 6:5 CEV), the vast majority of Christians today would not be concerned with slave-owners being out of a job. Yet, when it comes to harming animals, Christians are often more concerned about the workers than they are about the ethics of what their job entails.

Critics would be right to point out that crop workers are often exploited too. The growing and processing of vegetables and fruit depend on

7. King, *Meat: The New Cigarette*, 51–53.
8. King, *Meat: The New Cigarette*, 90.

a human workforce, primarily immigrants, including numerous undocumented. Crop work is often dangerous and difficult, as it involves heavy lifting, repetitive movements, and the operation of heavy machinery. Thus, this crop work carries an injury risk. The work is done outside in high temperatures, frequently without ample hydration or shade. Crop workers are also commonly exposed to harmful herbicides or pesticides, frequently without satisfactory protection. Additionally, the laborers are frequently underpaid, and higher-ups and coworkers sexually abuse and harass numerous female employees. Of course, it would be best to buy from local family farms or produce our own crops. However, this is not always practical or realistic for the average person. In addition, poor living situations, truncated salaries, and abuse of employees have been recorded on certain family farms. These farms sell at community-supported agricultural programs, well-liked farmers' markets, and farm-to-table eateries.[9]

Yet, we all have to eat, and there is no getting around it. When one cannot avoid harm, one can at least minimize it. Fortunately, veganism still causes the least damage as most crops are fed to farm animals before slaughter. Worldwide, 98 percent of total soy and 70 percent of total grain are eaten by farmed animals.[10] In other words, the vast majority of crops grown are not for vegans. With all of this information, it is clear that crop work needs to be reformed. However, the critical difference between crop work and meat-packing and slaughterhouses is that crop work is theoretically not as emotionally damaging. It is like that old vegan statement: "Would you rather take your kid to pick apples or to cut an animal up inside of a slaughterhouse?" Abattoirs are inherently damaging to the mind and frightening to witness. A worker does not have to turn off their natural sense of compassion to pick a strawberry; they do, however, when it comes to killing cows and pigs. Importantly, Christians do not have to pay slaughterhouse employees to work there. Abstention from meat would absolve a Christian's involvement of causing that worker to have a higher arrest rate for rape, sex offenses, violent crimes, and total arrests. Fortunately, the new covenant (Luke 22:20) came with a new interpretation method to help Christians with this problem.

9. "Labor and Workers."
10. "Vegans Exploit Crop Workers," para. 3.

5

Reinterpreting with the New Covenant

HOSEA 2:18 IS PART of the new covenant in Jesus' blood (Luke 22:20). With this new covenant (Heb 9:15) comes a new method of interpretation. Second Corinthians 3:5–6 states, "Not that we are sufficient in ourselves to claim anything as coming from us, but our sufficiency is from God, who has made us sufficient to be ministers of a new covenant, not of the letter but of the Spirit. For the letter kills, but the Spirit gives life." In *I Will Abolish the Bow*, I discussed the difference between the spirit of the law and the letter of the law. Enacting the letter of the law means obeying just what the actual words say. Following the spirit of the law means observing the broad intention and principle of the verse and thus applying it beyond to whom it was specified.[1]

For example, Deut 27:18 NASB condemns anyone who misleads a blind person. A Christian following the letter of the law would never mislead a blind person but still mislead someone who is deaf or physically disabled. A Christian following the spirit of the law would not mislead any disabled individual based on Deut 27:18 NASB. I think believers can now administer the spirit of the law to animals. This administration is made clear in 2 Cor 3:1–8, which implies that the spirit of the law began with the new covenant. The same new covenant Jesus started with his blood (Luke 22:20), and the new covenant mentioned in Hos 2:18. With this new interpretation method (2 Cor 3:5–6), Christians can reinterpret many passages that may have only explicitly applied to humans when written and now employ them towards animals. This chapter is in no way meant to

1. King, *I Will Abolish the Bow*, 70–72.

be exhaustive; thus, I will first reinterpret perhaps the most well-known of biblical ethical principles, the Ten Commandments (Exod 20:1–17).

Reinterpreting the Ten Commandments

Generally, the Ten Commandments (20:1–17) are thought to be still binding on Christians unless stated otherwise in the New Testament. When originally written, the Ten Commandments (20:1–17) were probably not intended for the consideration of animals. However, the new covenant brought the spirit of the law (2 Cor 3:5–6) interpretation method. Thus, I have written a reinterpretation of the Ten Commandments (Exod 20:1–17) using the spirit of the law (2 Cor 3:5–6). This reinterpretation will help Christians to align their actions with the new covenant of Hos 2:18 NIV, which implies a world where animals and humans will live in peace. I first list the principle of the commandment, where it can be found in the Bible, and the quoted verse. Then, I apply the commandment in a way that aligns with the new covenant of Hos 2:18.

1. **No Idols—Exod 20:3**
   "You shall have no other gods before me."
   Christian omnivores frequently make a god out of their eating habits. They often state that a life without steak or cheese is not worth living. Their gluttonous desires become an idol whom they serve daily with their meal choices. This idol is not even benevolent. Purchasing meat (and other animal products) leads to immense harm and suffering to animals, human health, and the environment. Christian omnivores remind me of Phil 3:18–19: "For many, of whom I have often told you and now tell you even with tears, walk as enemies of the cross of Christ. Their end is destruction, their god is their belly, and they glory in their shame, with minds set on earthly things." In context, Phil 3:18–19 may be talking about Judaizers (3:2 NLT). More likely, I think Phil 3:18–19 is talking about antinomians. These believers take God's gift of salvation by grace through faith (Eph 2:8) and use it to continue to sin (Rom 6:1–2). Regardless, the attitudes and behaviors of many Christian omnivores certainly match the description of Phil 3:18–19.

2. **No Creating, Worshiping, or Serving Graven Images—Exod 20:4–6**
"You shall not make for yourself a carved image, or any likeness of anything that is in heaven above, or that is in the earth beneath, or that is in the water under the earth. You shall not bow down to them or serve them, for I the LORD your God am a jealous God, visiting the iniquity of the fathers on the children to the third and the fourth generation of those who hate me, but showing steadfast love to thousands of those who love me and keep my commandments."

Nick Fiddes, a social anthropologist, states that meat is culturally esteemed because animal consumption traditionally signified human domination and power over nature. Similarly, Julia Twigg, a sociologist, and additional scholars state that meat is symbolic of strength and power and is linked with masculinity.[2] To my knowledge, Christians do not make statues out of animal flesh and worship or serve them. However, the principle of Exod 20:4–6 is not to create, worship, or serve idols instead of loving and following the commands of God. When Christians glorify the consumption of meat (like social media posts of flesh dinners), they create an idol and subconsciously worship the flesh to symbolize domination and power over the natural world. Christians may also serve this idol by defending meat and all of the destruction it causes with ridiculous arguments and rationalizations. Many Christians worship the idol by essentially tithing their money to the meat industry. I believe most Christians have made meat into an idol. Why else would they become so illogically defensive when confronted with its harm to human health, animals, and the environment? In my experience, most Christians cannot have a sensible discussion about meat without getting defensive. This defensiveness indicates that Christians have placed meat into a realm that is not to be questioned, above how believers are to even interact with God (Jas 1:5–6). Additionally, I see nothing about meat today that would indicate a Christian keeps God's commands or loves God.

3. **Do Not Take God's Name in Vain—Exod 20:7**
"You shall not take the name of the LORD your God in vain, for the LORD will not hold him guiltless who takes his name in vain."

I discussed this commandment in *I Will Abolish the Bow*. This commandment most significantly means not to use the name of God

---

2. Judge, "Social and Ideological Foundations," para. 4, 10.

to support or perpetuate evil.[3] Unfortunately, Christians frequently justify eating meat in the name of God and the Bible. This justification generally contributes to animal cruelty (Prov 12:10 NLT), environmental destruction (Num 35:33–34; Jer 2:7), infectious disease emergence (Num 11:31–34 NLT) and perpetuation, antibiotic resistance, food poisoning, resource wasting (John 6:11–12), chronic illnesses (Deut 7:15), and poor working conditions. These problems lead to much death, which God probably considers evil (1 Cor 15:26). These problems created by meat are likely not something God is happy about Christians justifying.

Additionally, meat is associated with evil in the Bible. For instance, eating animal flesh was only permitted (Gen 9:3–4) after the human heart was associated with evil intention (8:21). Similarly, in 1 Cor 10:3–6 NLT, it is said that the desert quail flesh-eaters of Num 11:4–34 NLT craved "evil things"—which is meat (11:31–34 NLT). Finally, on the new earth (Isa 65:17), it is said in Isa 11:9 GNT that nothing evil or harmful will occur between all sentient beings (11:6–8 GNT). All animals, including present omnivores and carnivores, will be strictly herbivorous (11:7; 65:25) on the new earth (66:22)—thus, there will be no meat-eating. One author stated it this way,

> Actually, these passages indicate very specifically that carnivorous activity is an evil—that is, a physical rather than a moral evil. The Hebrew word translated "hurt" in the KJV of Isaiah 11:9 and 65:25 is *raa*. Elsewhere in the Old Testament, the most frequent translation of this word is "do evil". Other translations include "afflict" and "do wickedly". It is related to *ra*, the usual word for "evil" in the Old Testament—and that includes both moral and physical evil. As for the word translated "destroy" in the KJV in Isaiah 11:9 and 65:25 (*shachath*), the core meaning is "mar" or "corrupt". No wonder carnivorous activity has no place in the new creation![4]

Therefore, Christians using God's name to justify and perpetuate an evil like meat-eating is to take God's name in vain (Exod 20:7).

4. Observe the Sabbath—Exod 20:8–11

"Remember the Sabbath day, to keep it holy. Six days you shall labor, and do all your work, but the seventh day is a Sabbath to the LORD

---

3. King, *I Will Abolish the Bow*, 42–43.
4. Gurney, "Carnivorous Nature," 70–75.

your God. On it you shall not do any work, you, or your son, or your daughter, your male servant, or your female servant, or your livestock, or the sojourner who is within your gates. For in six days the LORD made heaven and earth, the sea, and all that is in them, and rested on the seventh day. Therefore the LORD blessed the Sabbath day and made it holy."

The Sabbath commandment (20:8–11) may not be required for Christians, as Rom 14:5–6 and Col 2:16–17 seem to negate any mandates. Although some Christians and denominations interpret Rom 14:5–6 and Col 2:16–17 differently, thus believing the Sabbath commandment (Exod 20:8–11) is still required for believers. Regardless, agriculture today does not have much to do with the Sabbath. In biblical times, animals used on the farm (Deut 22:10) required Sabbath rest (5:14 NLT). However, at present, farm animal labor has largely been replaced by tractors and other technology. One could argue that animal agriculture workers may work on the Sabbath. Yet, harvesting plants may also involve Sabbath work. Realistically, it may be nearly impossible to know if the food we buy was produced on the Sabbath.

5. Honor Your Mother and Father—Exod 20:12

"Honor your father and your mother, that your days may be long in the land that the LORD your God is giving you."

Generally, meat contributes to environmental destruction (Num 35:33–34; Jer 2:7), infectious disease emergence (Num 11:31–34 NLT) and perpetuation, antibiotic resistance, food poisoning, resource wasting (John 6:11–12), chronic illnesses (Deut 7:15), and poor working conditions. Can Christians truly honor their mother and father when partaking in animal flesh? The Christian omnivore would be contributing to their mom or dad's antibiotics not working anymore or their sickness in the future from a pandemic. What if the Christian's mom or dad works at a slaughterhouse? The Christian's meat-eating would be why their parents suffer at that miserable job. Nothing about a Christian partaking in meat today honors their mother and father.

6. You Shall Not Murder—Exod 20:13

"You shall not murder."

As I mentioned in *I Will Abolish the Bow*, this commandment was probably written to apply exclusively to humans. However, through the spirit of the law (2 Cor 3:5–6), the Christian Animal

Rights Association also applies this commandment to animals.[5] A popular secular animal rights activist phrase is "meat is murder." If we apply the spirit of the law (3:5–6) to Exod 20:13 by applying it to animals, meat is most certainly murder and thus should be avoided.

7. **You Shall Not Commit Adultery—Exod 20:14**
"You shall not commit adultery."

Data collected from an adultery website indicated that New Zealanders looking for an affair were more likely to be smokers, meat-eaters, and Christians.[6] The Christian part certainly surprised me, as one would think they would follow the biblical teaching of Exod 20:14 and Matt 19:17–18, to name but a few. Several explanations may enlighten how these toxic personal behaviors, specifically meat-eating and smoking, are associated with adultery-seeking. Perhaps poor impulse control (Prov 25:28 NLT), culture (Rom 12:2), ignorance (1 Pet 1:14 NIV), selfishness (Rom 2:8 GNT), and bad decision-making (Prov 14:12) are at play. My possible explanations go beyond the data, though. Regardless, since some evidence indicates that meat-eating is associated with adultery-seeking, it may be best to avoid consuming flesh to minimize the chances of breaking Exod 20:14.

8. **You Shall Not Steal—Exod 20:15**
"You shall not steal."

Omnivorous humans, even vegetarians, are guilty of stealing the secretions of animals that were never intended for human consumption (Gen 1:29–30). For instance, humans steal milk from the breasts of cows, which were designed for their baby calves. Additionally, humans steal honey from the hardworking bees, who create, store, and then consume it during the winter. Along the same lines, animals own nothing beyond their own lives. Yet, humanity steals it from them when humans demand animal flesh. Then there is also the human aspect. Collective humanity indulges in meat, which generally contributes to environmental destruction (Num 35:33–34; Jer 2:7), infectious disease emergence (Num 11:31–34 NLT) and perpetuation, antibiotic resistance, food poisoning, resource wasting (John 6:11–12), and poor working conditions. This devastation is a thief to human health, well-being, and joy. Similarly, when one indulges in meat and other animal

5. King, *I Will Abolish the Bow*, 70–72.
6. "Infidelity."

products, they potentially feed chronic disease (Deut 7:15) to their bodies. They may steal joy, health, and even life from themselves. This destruction of personal health steals happiness from their loved ones when they see the omnivore sick in the hospital instead of living in wellness (3 John 1:2). Or even worse: the loved one is robbed of happiness when they have to face the omnivore's untimely death from the diseases caused by consuming meat and other animal products.

9. **You Shall Not Lie—Exod 20:16**
"You shall not bear false witness against your neighbor."

Exodus 20:16 primarily condemns perjury. Although, in principle, Exod 20:16 condemns general dishonesty. Indeed, Exod 20:16 CEV states, "Do not tell lies about others." Humans lie to themselves when they eat the flesh of animals and think that it is not causing harm to themselves, the animals, and generally other humans. Society perpetuates the lie by using euphemisms around food to help humanity feel better about their choices. For example, cow flesh becomes beef, and pig flesh becomes pork or bacon. Christians often outright deny animal agriculture's effects on the planet by dismissing climate change or minimizing its potential destruction. Christians essentially lie to themselves to keep eating their favorite treats, guilt-free. Also, most parents lie to their children about meat and its origins. Additionally, the animal agriculture industry lies in the promotion of its products. For example, milk marketing often depicts happy cows when the reality is much more gruesome. Similarly, meat marketing sometimes portrays comfortable animals but never the dreadful process of how the flesh gets to the store.

10. **You Shall Not Covet—Exod 20:17**
"You shall not covet your neighbor's house; you shall not covet your neighbor's wife, or his male servant, or his female servant, or his ox, or his donkey, or anything that is your neighbor's."

Though this commandment discusses the owning of humans and animals, the principle of Exod 20:17 NASB is not to intensely desire what belongs to someone else. As the wording implies, Exod 20:17 NASB almost certainly was written to only apply to free Israelite (20:2) men. However, utilizing the spirit of the law (2 Cor 3:5–6), we can use the principle of Exod 20:17 to criticize what humans do to animals. For instance, fast-food advertisements frequently depict meat and cheese in an enticing manner, essentially glamorizing the food. When humans stare at that embellished meat and cheese, they generally lose sight that the flesh and secretions belonged to someone else. Thus, through these advertisements, humans may covet the animals' flesh and secretions. Furthermore, another interpretation method similar to the spirit of the law (2 Cor 3:5–6) exists, which I call, "The Unity of Creation Principle."

The Unity of Creation Principle

Paul and Sosthenes (1 Cor 1:1) seemingly use the spirit of the law (2 Cor 3:5–6) in 1 Cor 9:9–10. Paul and Sosthenes (1:1) took a verse that was explicitly written about animals (Deut 25:4) and applied its principle to humans (1 Cor 9:9–10)—specifically, Christian preachers (9:14). I do the reverse with some verses that are expressly or most likely addressed to humans and apply their concepts to animals.[7] I named this interpretation method the "Unity of Creation Principle," which is essential in light of the new covenant because Hos 2:18 NIV says that *all* may safely rest. For example, in Matt 7:12, Jesus stated, "So whatever you wish that others would do to you, do also to them, for this is the Law and the Prophets." Similarly, in Luke 6:31, Jesus stated, "And as you wish that others would do to you, do so to them." When originally written, Matt 7:12 and Luke 6:31 were probably only regarding the treatment of humans.[8] However, using the Unity of Creation Principle (1 Cor 9:9–10), Christians can apply these golden rule verses (Matt 7:12; Luke 6:31) to animals, too. With virtually any verse concerning human justice, the Unity of Creation Principle (1 Cor 9:9–10) could be applied to animals, which reflects the new covenant of Hos 2:18 NIV. An obvious rebuttal to this reinterpretation of the golden rule (Matt 7:12; Luke 6:31) would be that Jesus virtually never applied it to animals. The next chapter attempts to explain why Jesus did not apply this ethical principle to animals.

7. King, *I Will Abolish the Bow*, 92–93.
8. King, *I Will Abolish the Bow*, 69.

6

Jesus and His Decisions as God

THE ONLY REASONABLE ARGUMENT against the new covenant of Hos 2:18, starting with the blood of Jesus (Mark 14:24), is that Christ did not show peace towards other creatures while he walked the earth—especially fish. Jesus fed about five thousand males with fish meat (and bread) (Matt 14:13–21; Mark 6:30–44; Luke 9:10–17; John 6:1–15). Later, Jesus fed about four thousand men with fish flesh (and bread) (Matt 15:32–39; Mark 8:1–10). Christ also helped his disciples catch fish. Jesus cooked fish, feeding their flesh to his disciples for breakfast (John 21:1–15). Jesus even feeds himself fish meat in Luke 24:41–43. In *I Will Abolish the Bow*, I reasoned that obtaining food in biblical times was not nearly as easy as today in the modern world.[1] Thus, I think it is safe to say that Jesus would be vegan today. Still, it does trouble me that Jesus was not vegan (or even vegetarian). Jesus' omnivory (24:41–43) bothers me because his principles (Mark 9:35; Luke 6:31), the garden of Eden (Gen 1:20—2:8), and the new earth (Isa 65:17–25) point to veganism being best. It troubles me that Jesus could have been vegan (or even vegetarian) and *not* cause harm to animals because he is God (John 10:30). Jesus could have just spontaneously created plants if he wanted to. Then again, maybe Jesus had a reason. This chapter focuses on the possible reasons that Jesus was not vegan (or vegetarian) despite the inauguration of the new covenant of Hos 2:18.

1. King, *I Will Abolish the Bow*, 64.

Do as They Say, Not as They Do

Regardless of why Jesus ate meat (Luke 24:41–43), this is not the only issue where God (John 10:30) told us an ideal yet did not live by it. For example, as I explained in *I Will Abolish the Bow*, Jesus told the Pharisees that divorce was given as a concession to deal with humanity's hardness of heart (Matt 19:1–8). Divorce was allowed (Deut 24:1) because humans could not keep the ideal God created in Eden (Gen 2:15) of an inseparable marriage (2:24).[2] Similarly, God explained the ideal of veganism in the garden of Eden (1:27—2:8). This vegan ideal of peaceful harmony between humans and animals (Isa 11:6–9) is seen again on the new earth (66:22) after Jesus returns (Matt 24:30). Like divorce, eating meat was allowed (Gen 9:3–4) as a concession to humanity's heart of evil intention (8:21). What always struck me as odd was that God showed us the ideal of veganism (1:27–31) and yet did not live up to it himself, as evidenced by Jesus (John 10:30) eating fish meat (Luke 24:41–43).

Yet, this is not the only time God did not live up to his ideal. For example, God married Israel (Jer 31:31–32; Ezek 16:3–8 GNT). Despite claiming to hate divorce (Mal 2:16 NASB), God divorced Israel (Jer 3:6–8 NLT). Postmillennial theologian Kenneth L. Gentry Jr. proposes that the document in Rev 5 is a decree of divorce that God gives to Israel for her adultery (Isa 1:21 NLT; Jer 3:6–8 NLT; Rev 17:1–2).[3] This adultery is symbolized by Hos 2:1–17, in which Israel was worshiping idols instead of God (2:13, 2:16–17). Hosea 2:19–23 then prophesies Jesus (John 10:30) marrying a reconstituted bride (Rom 11:13–24 NLT), the church (Eph 5:25; Rev 19:7–9; 21:2). God gave us a picture of the ideal regarding both meat and divorce yet did not live by it himself. Still, in John 14:12, Jesus said that believers would do greater works than him. Sandwiched between Hos 2:1–17 and Hos 2:19–23 is Hos 2:18 NIV, a declaration of a new covenant in which animals and humans will live in safety. As Christ's reconstituted bride, the church (Eph 5:25) has a responsibility to make Hos 2:18 a reality. Importantly, just like believers would not use God's divorce from Israel (Jer 3:6–8 NLT) to justify their own divorce, maybe Christians should not use Jesus (John 10:30) eating fish flesh (Luke 24:41–43) to justify themselves eating meat. Maybe God/Jesus (John 10:30) wants us to do as they say, not

2. King, *I Will Abolish the Bow*, 52.
3. Gentry, "God's Divorce Decree."

as they do. Regardless, maybe not eating meat in first-century Israel was just too difficult for the average person.

My Burden is Light

One possibility is that Jesus was not vegan (or vegetarian) because he was trying to get potential followers to submit to him without too much burden. For instance, Jesus said in Matt 11:28–30, "Come to me, all who labor and are heavy laden, and I will give you rest. Take my yoke upon you, and learn from me, for I am gentle and lowly in heart, and you will find rest for your souls. For my yoke is easy, and my burden is light." Being vegan (or vegetarian) in the first-century Mediterranean world was probably far from easy and probably a burden. Food scarcity was a real issue (6:25 NLT). Today, however, with fast-food restaurants and 24/7 supermarkets offering cruelty-free options, veganism is hardly a burden. Or maybe Jesus was leaving room for his followers to be even better in actions than him. Again, in John 14:12, Jesus stated, "Truly, truly, I say to you, whoever believes in me will also do the works that I do; and greater works than these will he do, because I am going to the Father." I think based on John 14:12, Jesus expected his followers to pick up where he left off and work towards restoring the world back to the paradise of Eden (Isa 51:3). That is why Jesus said to pray (Matt 6:9), "Your kingdom come, your will be done, on earth as it is in heaven" (6:10). As we see in prophecies about the new earth (Isa 65:17), God's ultimate will is that animals and humans live together in peace (11:6–9; Hos 2:18 NIV). Jesus said that anyone who does the will of his Father is his family member (Matt 12:50). Regardless, Jesus may have severely limited the types of meat he ate, and certainly the amount.

Jesus, the Pescatarian?

Before I discuss the type of meat Jesus ate, I must first note that the amount of meat that Jesus ate was likely far different from the amount eaten today. One reputable source states about ancient Israelite food habits, "Meat was not consumed on a regular basis by the average Israelite, so most stews were made from legumes and vegetables. . . . Legumes are a good source of vegetable protein, which was imperative in a society that ate little meat. . . . The preference for stews made from vegetables and legumes supports the idea that the average Israelite household depended on herds and only occasionally ate meat." Meat was reserved for particular events like a feast or a wedding.[4] This minimal meat-eating by the average ancient Israelite is a stark contrast to the modern world. Absurdly, the average American eats an estimated 274 pounds of flesh annually, not counting seafood or waste.[5] Indisputably, Jesus would have never eaten even close to the amount of meat consumed today. Actually, he may have only eaten fish flesh.

One enthusiast named Henry, whom I met at Pittsburgh Vegfest in 2021, made an excellent point about how the Bible never explicitly mentions Jesus incarnate eating or feeding others with any kind of meat except for fish. He thought that perhaps pescatarianism could be seen as biblically acceptable, while other forms of meat should be discouraged. First Corinthians 15:39 makes a distinction between the different types of flesh, stating, "For not all flesh is the same, but there is one kind for humans, another for animals, another for birds, and another for fish." Indeed, the Catholic Church has seemingly always made a distinction between the flesh of fish and the flesh of other animals. Hence, this distinction is why, to my knowledge, Catholics typically abstain from meat during Lent Fridays but still eat fish flesh. Based on 1 Cor 15:39, people in biblical times understood flesh as not being the same. I imagine that animal flesh is what humans would consider "red meat" today. Bird flesh is what humanity would commonly associate with "white meat." Finally, there is fish flesh. Fish meat was probably considered the healthiest of the three types of non-human flesh. I must admit that fish, in and of itself, is the healthiest flesh, as high red (may include processed) meat consumption is notoriously linked to health problems. Eating white meat is a little better for health, but is just as bad as eating red meat for cholesterol.[6] Consuming fish flesh (pescatarianism), however, has numerous health benefits when compared to meat-eaters.[7] Thus, based on the health aspect, perhaps Jesus was advocating that fish should be seen as the only acceptable meat. That could be why Jesus fed others (Matt 14:13–21, 15:32–39; Mark 6:30–44, 8:1–10; Luke 9:10–17; John 6:1–15, 21:1–15) and himself (Luke 24:41–43) with the flesh of fish.

Maybe Jesus fed others and himself with fish meat because the aquatic creatures do not experience pain. There is evidence that fish sense pain in a

---

4. Shafer-Elliott, "Daily Stew?"

5. Christen, "Meat Consumption in the U.S.," para. 2.

6. King, *Meat: The New Cigarette*, 24–27.

7. King, *Meat: The New Cigarette*, 64.

comparable form as humans do.[8] However, one study suggested that fish do not experience pain like humans.[9] Despite the conflicting evidence, I think the most rational reason Jesus fed others and himself with fish meat probably had to do with cost. Indeed, Bible scholar William Robertson Smith (AD 1846–1894) commented on biblical eating habits, stating, "Flesh of domestic animals was eaten only as a luxury or in times of famine."[10] However, fish were commonly eaten in biblical times. In contrast, the flesh of land animals was typically consumed only by the wealthy.[11] Back then, it seems that fish meat was not considered a luxury like land animal flesh. Fish meat was considered the food of the underprivileged, and Jesus was poor (2 Cor 8:9). Fish were probably abundant in aqueous places where Jesus visited, such as the Jordan River (Matt 3:13 NLT), the Mediterranean shore (15:21), and the Sea of Galilee (4:18 NLT).[12] It seems that the only time the Bible may imply that Jesus incarnate ate land animal flesh was the required yearly (Exod 12:1–28) Passover lamb (Luke 2:41–42 NLT; 22:7–15). As Henry pointed out, there is no explicit mention in the Bible that Jesus incarnate ate or fed others with any dead animal flesh besides fish. Jesus' behavior could perhaps be an implicit biblical endorsement of pescatarianism, and thus other forms of meat should be discouraged. This pescatarianism of Jesus would also fit with the surrounding community. One reputable source states, "People back in Jesus' time ate a mostly plant-based, clean diet. In that region of the world, lentils, whole grains, fruits, vegetables, dates, nuts and fish were all quite popular. . . . Furthermore, Jacobs and Colbert believe not only that the people of Jesus' time ate a more plant-based diet, they also think that our bodies were designed to eat a mostly plant-based diet—similar to what Jesus ate."[13]

Some Christians may wonder if they should consider pescatarianism because of Jesus. However, the possible pescatarianism of Jesus was likely tempered with the kosher restriction of only eating meat from fish with fins and scales (Lev 11:9–12; Deut 14:9–10). This restriction would severely limit the types of seafood that world cultures commonly eat. Additionally, today's fishing industry hardly looks like it did in biblical times. Fish then

8. Duncan, "Fish Can Feel Pain."

9. "Do Fish Feel Pain?"

10. Tibbetts, *Christian Insight*, 98.

11. King, *I Will Abolish the Bow*, 64.

12. Zavada, "What Would Jesus Eat?," para. 6.

13. "What Would Jesus Eat? The Science," paras. 2, 5.

were wild-caught. Today, fish are frequently farmed in what is known as aquaculture, which in its most horrific form is the marine parallel of factory farming. Fish are typically cramped and closely crowded, with little room to swim freely. This crowding may cause wounds and injuries to the fish. This stressful and congested environment causes diseases to thrive. Thus, pesticides and antibiotics are utilized to control the disease. This irresponsible use of the latter can instigate or worsen antibiotic resistance. Even wild-caught fish today are not the same as fish in biblical times.

Today, wild fish are often polluted with mercury. Activities like coal-burning for electricity, waste incineration, and smelting create mercurial byproducts which pollute the air. This floating mercury then settles into waterways which eventually ends up in the ocean. That oceanic mercury is then unknowingly consumed by the small fish. The bigger fish then consume the mercury-laden smaller fish, polluting themselves with mercury. Thus, humans who frequently eat the meat of wild-caught fish are at risk of mercury poisoning.[14] Based on the vast differences between the fishing industry today and the fishing industry when he walked the earth, would Jesus feed himself or others fish meat today? Likewise, would Jesus want Christians to eat fish flesh today? Indeed, the way most fish are treated in horrifying aquaculture today would qualify as animal cruelty, which is condemned in Prov 12:10 NLT. Additionally, based on 3 John 1:2, I doubt that the pollution of wild fish with mercury or farmed fish with pesticides and antibiotics would be something embraced by Jesus! Regardless, another popular theory is that perhaps Luke 24:41–43 (the passage where Jesus eats fish meat) was an allegory.

Jesus Ate Fish Flesh—An Allegory?

Another possibility is that Jesus eating fish meat is actually an allegory. As any Bible-believing Christian knows, the Bible is filled with all sorts of allegory, symbolism, metaphor, and other literary devices that are not to be taken literally. There are many Christians that stick to a strict literal interpretation of the Bible in an attempt to be logically consistent. I am not one of them, simply because there is too much within the Bible that is obviously not meant to be taken literally. For instance, the book of Revelation has all kinds of bizarre descriptions that do not make sense if taken plainly. Thus, when I read the Bible, I am always open to a possible metaphorical

14. King, *Meat: The New Cigarette*, 64–65.

53

understanding of the verse rather than literal, depending on the context and situation. Jesus eating fish meat (Luke 24:41–43) has historically also been read as allegory. Therefore, there is also the possibility that Jesus did not eat the flesh of fish at all. The Portuguese Catholic priest Saint Anthony of Padua (AD 1195–1231) thought that Jesus eating fish meat was an allegory. Similarly, Christian scholar Henry Karlson expanded on the idea, stating,

> It is also possible, following and developing upon what St. Anthony said, to consider the fish to represent humanity (and the whole of creation) which was be taken up by Christ. Peter and Andrew were called to become the fisher of men: fish, then, can serve as a symbol for those who have been converted and handed over to Christ. The fish, after all, was the symbol early Christians used to represent themselves as a sign of their faith. There could, therefore, be a symbolic meaning to the text itself, where the early readers understood themselves to be the broiled fish given over to Christ, who then willingly takes them into himself and renders them to eternal rest in him.[15]

Although this is certainly a creative interpretation of Luke 24:41–43, I do not think the context or the situation indicates that the passage is meant to be taken as solely allegorical or metaphorical. Regardless, another important factor on what Jesus ate has to do with how the Bible has been altered over time.

Translations and Additions

Before I start, I want to establish that I and the Christian Animal Rights Association believe the sixty-six-book Bible—which consists of the Old and New Testaments—to be God's authoritative and inspired word (2 Tim 3:16–17).[16] We believe, however, that this only applies to the *original* Bible that was completed perhaps within the first century AD, not long after the death of Christ. That original manuscript is long deteriorated and what is left is many copies of copies and multiple translations of those copies. Thus, this following section is mere speculation on my part about the biblical narrative that have either been perhaps wrongly translated or added later, maybe even long after the original manuscript was formed and completed.

---

15. Karlson, "Did the Post-Resurrection Jesus," para. 9–11.

16. King, "Statement of Faith," para. 1.

If enough evidence exists that a passage or entity within Scripture is a later addition, then it can be dismissed as inauthentic and unauthoritative.

Jesus Ate Fish . . . or the Honeycomb?

Importantly, the sole passage where Jesus ate meat (fish), Luke 24:41–43, has an interesting case of differing depending on the manuscript. For instance, most modern translations say that the disciples offered fish flesh to Jesus in Luke 24:41–42. However, some translations of Luke 24:42, like the KJB, NKJV, ABPE, DRB, LSV, WEB, and the YLT, add honeycomb to the fish the disciples gave Jesus to eat. These translations of Luke 24:41–42 say that the disciples offered Jesus fish meat *and* honeycomb. Some of these translations of Luke 24:43 that include the fish flesh *and* honeycomb (ABPE, DRB, LSV, WEB, YLT) seem to indicate that Jesus ate both. However, in the KJB and the NKJV, Luke 24:43 says that Jesus ate *it* in front of the disciples (not *them*). The KJB and NKJV leave open the question of whether Jesus chose to eat either the honeycomb *or* the fish meat, but it was not both. The differences in translations that include the honeycomb can be explained by pastor Frank L. Hoffman, who states, "The Greek really doesn't say either 'it' or 'these'. They have been added by translators for clarification. The Greek says: 'And taking before them, He ate.' What did He eat? We don't really know. It could have been either or both."[17] Additionally, some translations of Luke 24:42 like the ESV, BSB, BLB, CSB, and HCSB, include the honeycomb in a footnote. Regardless, is the honeycomb authentic? KJB defender Will Kinney states that the honeycomb of Luke 24:42 is present in many early manuscripts and is mentioned in commentary by early church fathers such as Justin Martyr (c. AD 100–c. 165), Tertullian (c. AD 155–c. 220), and Athanasius (c. AD 296–373).[18] There is good evidence to believe that the honeycomb of Luke 24:42 is authentic. Thus, in Luke 24:41–43 NKJV, there is good evidence that the disciples presented both a piece of fish flesh and some honeycomb to Jesus and that Jesus ultimately selected and ate the honeycomb and *not* the fish meat piece. Now granted, the honeycomb would not be vegan, but it would have been a more humane choice than the flesh of fish. The honeycomb would be vegetarian, though, as it is made of beeswax. Choosing and eating the honeycomb instead of the

---

17. Hoffman, "Luke 24:41–43," para. 7.
18. Kinney, "'And of an Honeycomb' (Luke 24:42)."

piece of fish meat would align with Jesus' character, as he is known as the "Prince of Peace" (Isa 9:6).

Alternate Translation of Luke 21:34-36

The original Hebrew, Greek, and Aramaic that the Bible was written in were not as smoothly translated as tradition likes us to believe. For instance, there is some biblical evidence that Jesus frowned upon meat, which is consistent with God's ideal of veganism seen explicitly in Eden (Gen 1:20— 2:8) and implied (Isa 11:6-9) on the new earth (66:22). Importantly, in an alternate reading of Luke 21:34-36 from an old Syriac manuscript of the Gospels called the *Evangelion da-Mepharreshe*, Jesus states, "Now beware in yourselves that your hearts do not become heavy with the eating of flesh and with the intoxication of wine and with the anxiety of the world, and that day come up upon you suddenly; for as a snare it will come upon all them that sit on the surface of the earth."[19] Jesus may have paraphrased Prov 23:20-21 with this alternate passage. The *Evangelion da-Mepharreshe* is a Syriac translation of the four Gospels, which were written originally in Greek. The *Evangelion da-Mepharreshe* is dated around AD 200,[20] making it a very early translation. Syriac is a dialect of the Aramaic language. Aramaic is widely believed to be the primary language that Jesus spoke while he walked the earth. Thus, this Syriac rendering of Luke 21:34-36 is perhaps an authentic quote from Jesus. However, the ESV translation (based on Greek) of Luke 21:34-35 states, "But watch yourselves lest your hearts be weighed down with dissipation and drunkenness and cares of this life, and that day come upon you suddenly like a trap. For it will come upon all who dwell on the face of the whole earth." I have not found a sufficient reason why Luke 21:34-36 of the Syriac *Evangelion da-Mepharreshe* criticizes meat-eating but the Greek of Luke 21:34-35 does not. Regardless, based on alternate translations of the Bible, Jesus may have abstained from meat (and criticized eating it), but what about when Jesus fed others fish meat?

---

19. Burkitt, *Evangelion da-Mepharreshe Volume I*, 395.

20. Burkitt, *Evangelion da-Mepharreshe Volume II*, 5.

Jesus Feeding the Five Thousand with Fish—A Later Addition?

Probably everyone that ever attended a church knows that Jesus fed about five thousand men with five loaves of bread and the meat of two fish (Matt 14:13–21; Mark 6:30–44; Luke 9:10–17; John 6:1–15). Jesus feeding the crowds (Matt 14:19) in this situation with fish is understandable as three of the four Gospels describe the area as "desolate" (14:15; Mark 6:35; Luke 9:12). The Merriam-Webster dictionary defines desolate as "barren" or "lifeless."[21] I think it is obvious, then, that the place had minimal vegetation. This situation would be reasonable to feed the crowd (9:16) fish, and would be the total opposite of the gluttony of meat criticized in the Bible (Num 11:31–34 NLT; Prov 23:20–21). Additionally, these fish were most likely already dead, so I think Jesus probably would have just multiplied the flesh without further killing. Sparing the fish further suffering and death would align with Jesus' character, as he is known as the "Prince of Peace" (Isa 9:6).

However, there is solid evidence that Jesus did not actually feed the five thousand with any fish. Some early Christian writers, including Arnobius (AD 255–330), Eusebius (c. AD 260–339), and Irenaeus (c. AD 130–c. 202), all discuss Jesus feeding the five thousand with bread but with no mention of fish. Even in a backward reference, Jesus does not mention fish. For example, in Matt 16:9, Jesus states, "Do you not yet perceive? Do you not remember the five loaves for the five thousand, and how many baskets you gathered?" Similarly, in Mark 8:18–19, Jesus states, "Having eyes do you not see, and having ears do you not hear? And do you not remember? When I broke the five loaves for the five thousand, how many baskets full of broken pieces did you take up?" Although, in context, Jesus was using a metaphor about leaven, telling his disciples (Matt 16:5) to beware of the teachings of the Sadducees and Pharisees (16:6, 11–12). Jesus also uses leaven as a metaphor to criticize Herod and the hypocrisy (Luke 12:1) of the Pharisees (Mark 8:15). Thus, Jesus may not have had a reason to mention the fish in the backward reference. Regardless, scholar Keith Akers thinks that the fish are a later insertion[22] that were not present in the original formed and completed Bible. I believe enough compelling evidence exists to say that Akers is correct. For further confirmation, in John 6:26, Jesus states, "Truly, truly, I say to you, you are seeking me, not because you

---

21. "Desolate."
22. Bean, "Evidence That Jesus."

saw signs, but because you ate your fill of the loaves." Again, no mention of fish. Although, in context, Jesus metaphorically describes himself as bread (6:27–58) and may not have had a reason to mention the fish. Regardless, enough evidence exists to declare that the fish was perhaps a later addition to Matt 14:13–21, Mark 6:30–44, Luke 9:10–17, and John 6:1–15 and is thus inauthentic and unauthoritative.

Jesus Feeding the Four Thousand with Fish—A Later Addition?

There is also the miracle of Jesus feeding about four thousand men with seven loaves of bread and the meat of a few little fish (Matt 15:32–39; Mark 8:1–10). Jesus feeding the crowd (Matt 15:35; Mark 8:1) in this situation with fish is again understandable as both Gospels describe the area as "desolate" (Matt 15:33; Mark 8:4). Jesus even stated in Matt 15:32, "I have compassion on the crowd because they have been with me now three days and have nothing to eat. And I am unwilling to send them away hungry, lest they faint on the way." Jesus said something similar in Mark 8:2–3. Again, this situation would be totally reasonable for Jesus to feed the crowd (Matt 15:35; Mark 8:6) fish and would be the total opposite of the gluttony of meat criticized in the Bible (Num 11:31–34 NLT; Prov 23:20–21). Additionally, these fish were most likely already dead, so I think Jesus probably would have just multiplied the flesh without further killing. Sparing the fish further suffering and death would align with Jesus' character, as he is known as the "Prince of Peace" (Isa 9:6). Importantly, Jesus again makes a backward reference and makes no mention of the fish being there. Jesus states in Matt 16:10, "Or the seven loaves for the four thousand, and how many baskets you gathered?" Similarly, in Mark 8:20, Jesus states, "And the seven for the four thousand, how many baskets full of broken pieces did you take up?" Could it also be that the fish was a later addition in this instance too? Although, in context, Jesus was using a metaphor about leaven, telling his disciples (Matt 16:5) to beware of the teachings of the Sadducees and Pharisees (16:6; 16:11–12). Jesus also uses leaven as a metaphor to criticize Herod and the hypocrisy (Luke 12:1) of the Pharisees (Mark 8:15). Thus, Jesus may not have had a reason to mention the fish in the backward reference. Regardless, because of the parallel to when Jesus fed the five thousand (Matt 14:13–21; Mark 6:30–44; Luke 9:10–17; John 6:1–15), I think there is some evidence to declare that the fish was perhaps a later addition to Matt 15:32–39; Mark 8:1–10 and is thus inauthentic and unauthoritative.

Jesus Feeding the Disciples with Fish—A Later Addition?

Jesus fed fish meat to his disciples in John 21:1–15. After his resurrection (21:14), Jesus appeared to his disciples (21:1, 14) and helped them catch fish (21:6, 10–11); shortly after, he cooked the fish and served the meat with toasted bread (21:9, 13) for breakfast (21:12, 15). There is no mention of this pericope occurring in a "desolate" place like the previous feedings of fish. However, like Mark 16:9–20, John 21 has had its authenticity questioned. Christianity scholar Helmut Koester (AD 1926–2016) states that all of John 21 is extensively acknowledged as a later inclusion, even though it is present in every existing manuscript. He adds that John 20:30–31 is the Gospel's original ending, which is exaggeratively reiterated in John 21:25.[23] While discussing the Gospel of John, blogger Scott Bignell states, "I think there once existed a source that concluded with 20:30–31, and that chapter 21 was added onto that at a later time." Bignell declares this after pointing out that John 20:30–31 seems like the Gospel's conclusion. Bignell also points out that many expressions and words are only seen in John 21 but not the Gospel's prior chapters. I think this inconsistency may imply a different author wrote John 21 than the rest of the Gospel. Additionally, Scott notes that an early manuscript of John finishes chapter 20 but leaves a large amount of blank space before beginning chapter 21 on the next page. This blank space is an irregularity, as the remainder of the manuscript displays no inclination to start novel pericopes upon brand-new pages. Also, a certain fourth-century manuscript may conclude at John 20:31. Likewise, Bignell reports that in *Against Praxeas*, author Tertullian (c. AD 155–c. 220) appears to imply that the Gospel of John he was reading ended at 20:31. Although, there is evidence to the contrary. Importantly, Bignell states, "John 21 is probably not original to the fourth Gospel. It is likely an addition to a text that initially ended at John 20:31."[24] However, not all scholars agree and believe that John 21 is authentic. Regardless, I think there is enough evidence to declare that John 21:1–25 is perhaps a later addition and thus is inauthentic and unauthoritative. However, no evidence exists that Luke 5:1–11 is inauthentic. Luke 5:1–11 describes a similar but separate account of Jesus helping three

---

23. Koester, *Introduction to the New Testament*, 192.
24. Bignell, "John 21."

of his future apostles (Matt 10:2) catch many fish. Although the reader is left to wonder what happened to the fish that were caught in Luke 5:1–11, as there is no indication that they were later eaten. Luke 5:10–11 indicates that Simon, John, and James left their fishing gear behind and followed Jesus. Maybe they threw the fish back in the water? Regardless, beyond translation and additions, sources outside of the Bible also can tell us more about Jesus' interactions with and teachings about food.

Extrabiblical Sources

There is some extrabiblical evidence that Jesus abstained from meat. Much of this is from an early Christian group known as the Ebionites. They rejected Paul's epistles and considered him a false apostle. The Ebionites continued following the Hebrew religious and dietary laws. They likely rejected various mainstream fundamental Christian doctrines. For instance, the Ebionites believed that Jesus was not God incarnate (Phil 2:5–6) or the Messiah (John 4:26 NLT), but rather the mortal genetic son of Joseph and Mary and a holy prophet regarding the kingdom of heaven. The Ebionites also likely denied the birth of Jesus from a virgin (Matt 1:18–25), the atonement (1 John 4:10 NIV), and the Trinity (Matt 28:19). Their only canon was the Old Testament and the Gospel of the Hebrews. The latter was an Aramaic rendition of the Gospel of Matthew, which reportedly excluded the opening two chapters (Jesus' nativity).[25] The Ebionite version of the Gospel of the Hebrews was called the Gospel of the Ebionites.[26] I reject most of these theological issues because they conflict with the Bible (Ps 12:6 NIV). Although, I will focus on the Hebrew religious and dietary laws (such as Lev 11:1–47 and Deut 14:1–21) in the next chapter.

Importantly, the Ebionites acknowledged that Jesus invited Christians to live in alignment with the ideals seen in the coming kingdom, the new earth (Isa 65:17–25). They believed Jesus' ministry ushered in the beginning of the kingdom of God (Mark 1:15) that would be completed in its entirety (Dan 2:44) by a future Messiah. Although, the Bible declares that Jesus is this Messiah (Matt 1:16 NLT). However, the Ebionite belief of "inaugurated eschatology" with the kingdom of God (Acts 28:31) being "here/already, but not yet" (Heb 2:8 NLT)[27] fits with our ministry's postmillennial

25. "Ebionites."
26. Bean, "Evidence That Jesus."
27. "Ebionites."

interpretation of Scripture.[28] The Ebionite belief of "inaugurated eschatology" similarly closely resembles my thesis on the new covenant of Hos 2:18.
They were also theologically correct based on what Jesus said in Matt 6:10,
"Your kingdom come, your will be done, on earth as it is in heaven." This
theology would help explain why the Ebionites were purportedly vegetarians that opposed sacrificing animals.[29] They probably were living by the
ideals of the future new earth (Isa 65:17), where humans and animals will
live in peaceful harmony, without harm or death (11:6–9) for all eternity
(65:18). Most significantly, the Ebionites tell a different tale about Jesus'
lifestyle habits. These habits can, at first, be seen when examining the biblical requirement to annually kill the Passover lamb and eat his flesh (Exod
12:1–28). Jesus never disobeyed the law (Heb 4:14–15). Thus, during his
life, Jesus would have eaten this Passover lamb flesh (implied by Luke
2:41–42 NLT), as it was mandatory (Exod 12:1–28). Thus, we will assume
that there was a dead lamb present at the final Passover (Luke 22:7–16) and
that Jesus may have eaten the flesh. Or did he?

Jesus Rejected the Passover Lamb?

Jesus' death fulfilled and ended (1 Cor 5:7 CEV) the previous requirement
to annually kill and eat the flesh of the Passover lamb (Exod 12:1–28).[30] Jesus established the Lord's Supper in place of the Passover (Luke 22:15–20).[31]
The institution of the Lord's Supper may have been out of concern for the
sheep, as the Gospel of the Ebionites reports Jesus stating, "I have no desire
to eat the flesh of this Paschal Lamb with you."[32] This vegan-friendly quote
is in contrast to Luke 22:15, which reports Jesus as stating, "I have earnestly
desired to eat this Passover with you before I suffer." A Jesus who did not
want to eat the lamb flesh would make more sense as to why he abolished (1
Cor 5:7 CEV) the requirement (Exod 12:1–28). These contradicting quota-
tions were written around the same time. The Gospel of the Ebionites is
dated between AD 100 and 160.[33] The Gospel of Luke is dated between AD

---

28. King, "Organizational Theology."

29. "Ebionites."

30. King, *I Will Abolish the Bow*, 65.

31. King, *I Will Abolish the Bow*, 81.

32. Bean, "Evidence That Jesus," para. 39.

33. Kirby, "Gospel of the Ebionites."

80 and 130.[34] The Bible claims itself to be infallible (2 Sam 22:31 NIV; Pss 12:6 NIV; 19:7–8; 33:4 NIV; Prov 30:5 NIV; 2 Pet 1:19 NIV); thus, it cannot be wrong. Biblical infallibility makes sense because its author (2 Tim 3:16–17) is infallible (Deut 32:4 NLT; Matt 5:48). Thus, believers would have to declare the Gospel of the Ebionites quote as fabricated. Indeed, Bishop Epiphanius (c. AD 315–403) seems to have thought that Jesus' Gospel of the Ebionites quote is an alteration of Luke 22:15.[35] Although, Epiphanius was not infallible. Thus, could both quotes be authentic? The early dating of both suggests so.

Perhaps Jesus was being sarcastic in Luke 22:15. When juxtaposed with his Gospel of the Ebionites quote, I can definitely imagine Jesus sarcastically saying, "I have earnestly desired to eat this Passover with you before I suffer." Jesus was sarcastic in Luke 13:33 NIV, stating that no prophet can perish outside of Jerusalem. Yet, Heb 13:12 NLT declares that Jesus suffered and died outside of Jerusalem. Therefore, Jesus was a prophet (Matt 21:11) that died outside of Jerusalem. Jesus knew that he would perish outside of Jerusalem because he knows everything (John 16:29–31). Thus, in Luke 13:33 NIV, Jesus was being morbidly sarcastic! Jesus just might have been sarcastic in Luke 22:15 when speaking about the possible lamb corpse present at the final Passover (22:7–16). It is possible to harmonize the two conflicting quotes too. The NIV, NLT, and NASB of Luke 22:14–15 indicate that Jesus was eager to eat the Passover with his apostles. Why was he eager? Based on his statement in the Gospel of the Ebionites, Jesus' eagerness does not seem to have been over eating the lamb's flesh. Perhaps Jesus did not desire to eat the Passover lamb flesh but was eager to eat the other Passover fixings, like bitter herbs and unleavened bread (Exod 12:8). Beyond its basic necessity, eating also functions as a human social activity. Perhaps Jesus did not want to eat the Passover lamb flesh but desired fellowship with his apostles (Luke 22:14) because he knew he was soon going to suffer (22:15) and die (23:46). Perhaps Jesus was eager because he was hungry or for another reason that had nothing at all to do with food. These theories might explain why Jesus said he was eager (NIV, NLT, NASB) to eat the Passover with his apostles but did not specifically mention "meat" or "flesh" in Luke 22:14–15. Jesus might not have specifically said "meat" or "flesh" because there may not have even been a lamb corpse present at the final Passover (22:7–16).

34. Kirby, "Gospel of Luke."
35. Epiphanius, *Panarion*, 150.

A Passover without the Lamb?

Another possibility is that Jesus' final Passover took place without the lamb. Pope Benedict XVI (AD 1927–2022) said, "In all likelihood [Jesus] celebrated the Passover with his disciples in accordance with the Qumran calendar, hence, at least one day earlier; he celebrated it without a lamb, like the Qumran community which did not recognize Herod's temple and was waiting for the new temple."[36] Deuteronomy 16:5–6 required the Passover lamb to be sacrificially slaughtered at the temple. Therefore, Jesus would not have sinned by not eating lamb at Passover, because there was no legitimate temple. Thus, there was no lawful place to sacrificially slaughter the lamb. This thought may explain why there is no explicit mention of a lamb corpse at the final Passover involving Jesus and his apostles (Matt 26:17–25; Mark 14:12–21; Luke 22:7–16). Although, Jesus seemed to believe that the temple was legitimate (John 2:13–16). Mark 14:12 NIV and Luke 22:7 hint that a lamb was to be sacrificed for the final Passover. Again, Deut 16:5–6 indicates that the Passover lamb was required to be sacrificially slaughtered at the temple. However, no mention is made about a temple visit before the final Passover (Matt 26:17–25; Mark 14:12–21; Luke 22:7–16). Surprisingly, at that time, not all Jewish sects observed Passover by slaughtering the lamb. The Sadducees did, and perhaps the Pharisees too, but the Essenes did not. The Essenes rejected sacrificing animals, particularly citing Isa 1:11, Jer 7:22–24, and Zech 11:4–6. Importantly, Jesus criticized the teachings of the Sadducees and Pharisees (Matt 16:6–12). However, I have found no evidence or documentation that Jesus ever criticized or opposed the Essenes.[37] Jesus may have agreed with the Essenes.

The Gospel of the Ebionites has Jesus stating, "I am come to do away with sacrifices, and if you cease not sacrificing, the wrath of God will not cease from you."[38] Jesus may have wanted to stop animal sacrifices out of concern for the animals. The Bible seems to indicate this as Jesus said in John 10:11, "I am the good shepherd. The good shepherd lays down his life for the sheep." Although, in context, this quote symbolizes Jesus atoning for human sin (1 John 2:1–2 NLT), and thus human salvation (John 10:9). Additionally, Jesus referenced the words of Hos 6:6 NIV, stating that God desires mercy, not sacrifice (Matt 9:13, 12:7). Although in context, Jesus is

---

36. Bean, "Evidence That Jesus."
37. "Did Jesus Eat Lamb?," para. 2–4.
38. Bean, "Evidence That Jesus."

talking about God preferring ethical conduct (like mercy) instead of meaningless or legalistic religious behavior. Pointless religious behavior included not eating with sinners and tax collectors (9:11). Legalistic religious behavior included not working on the Sabbath (12:1–2). However, a broader application of Matt 9:13, 12:7, and John 10:11 would concern animals, as Jesus' sacrificial death eternally ceased animal sacrifices (Heb 10:12–18).[39] Ultimately, lamb may not have been present at the final Passover because it would have been redundant. Jesus symbolized the lamb (John 1:29, 36) that was sacrificed (1 Cor 5:7).

Jesus Taught Vegetarianism—and Maybe Even Was a Vegetarian

There is even evidence that Jesus taught others to be vegetarian. In his book, the bishop Epiphanius (c. AD 315–403) states, "Whenever you speak to them (Ebionites) concerning flesh food, the Ebionites reply they were vegetarian because 'Christ revealed it to me.'"[40] The Ebionites claimed that this was a direct teaching from Jesus himself, not some mystical revelation.[41] Jesus teaching vegetarianism would make sense, as he encouraged individuals to work towards the ideals of Eden (with marriage in Matt 19:1–12)[42] and the new earth (6:9–10).[43] Plus, Jesus' ethical teachings of the golden rule (7:12), loving your neighbor as yourself (22:39), and servanthood (Mark 9:35) are all consistent with refraining from harming animals.[44] If Jesus was teaching vegetarianism, why wouldn't he be vegetarian himself? It wouldn't make sense for him to advocate for others to live that way if he was not living that way himself.

There is indirect evidence that Jesus was a vegetarian. Eusebius (c. AD 260–339) states in *Ecclesiastical History* 2.23 that the Lord's brother, James (Gal 1:19), was brought up as a vegetarian.[45] If James grew up as a vegetarian, that would mean that his parents, Mary and Joseph (Matt 1:18–19; 13:53–55), were also most likely vegetarians. What parents would raise two

39. King, *I Will Abolish the Bow*, 72–73.

40. Tibbetts, *Christian Insight*, 23.

41. Cousens, *Conscious Eating*, 381.

42. Keener, "Jesus Summons Us."

43. King, *I Will Abolish the Bow*, 86–88.

44. King, *I Will Abolish the Bow*, 18–20.

45. Bean, "Evidence That Jesus."

kids with different dietary habits? Thus, it could be inferred that Jesus was raised as a vegetarian. Jesus may have been a vegetarian throughout his life, hence why he taught the Ebionites to live that way. Perhaps Jesus also taught his apostles to abstain from meat. That would explain why in *Demonstratio Evangelica* (Proof of the Gospels), Eusebius (c. AD 260–339) said that the apostles abstained from meat.[46] It seems odd that the apostles and many early church fathers were vegetarian but somehow the leader missed the message. Jesus' possible vegetarianism would explain why he criticized flesh-eating in the Syriac *Evangelion da-Mepharreshe* translation of Luke 21:34–36.[47] Additionally, Jesus' possible vegetarianism would further support the idea that Jesus chose and ate the honeycomb and *not* the fish meat piece in Luke 24:41–43 NKJV. Although this is not conclusive, as Jesus may have eaten both or chose to eat the fish meat and not the honeycomb. Nonetheless, what Jesus ate may be irrelevant, mostly because he can do what he wants because he is God (John 10:30).

Jesus and His Decisions as God

The subject of what Jesus ate must be put in context that he is not just a typical human being. Jesus is both fully God (John 17:21) and fully human (1 John 4:2). Regardless of how Jesus ate, this does not necessarily give us the right to do so. Jesus is God (Titus 2:13) and one with the Father (John 10:30). Psalms 50:10–11 and 104:24 declare that God (50:7) owns all creatures. That means that Jesus is allowed to take life whenever he pleases because he is the Creator. Job 1:21 HCSB famously proclaims that the Lord gives and also takes away. God can give and take life as God wishes. We do not have that freedom or right to do so. Deuteronomy 32:39 NIV makes this clear, as God states (32:36–37 NIV), "See now that I myself am he! There is no god besides me. I put to death and I bring to life, I have wounded and I will heal, and no one can deliver out of my hand."

The Divinity and Lordship of Jesus

Remembering that Jesus is ultimately God (2 Pet 1:1) troubles me less when I consider why he possibly fed fish meat to others (Matt 14:13–21,

---

46. Bean, "Evidence That Jesus."
47. Burkitt, *Evangelion da-Mepharreshe Volume I*, 395.

15:32–39; Mark 6:30–44, 8:1–10; Luke 9:10–17; John 6:1–15, 21:1–15), or possibly ate a piece of fish meat himself (Luke 24:41–43 NKJV). Ceasing from killing animals is a recognition that humans are not God. Though humans are made in God's image (Gen 1:26–27), humanity must let go of the idea that they are gods of all creation that can decide who can live and who can die. Finite humans do not have the absolute right to determine who lives and dies. However, the Creator, God himself, can decide—just like God does every day.

It is also important to recognize Jesus' divinity and lordship in his seemingly insensitive treatment of animals. For instance, Jesus permitted multiple demons to possess around two thousand pigs, with the pigs eventually drowning (Matt 8:28–34; Mark 5:1–20; Luke 8:26–39). Additionally, Jesus helped his disciples to fish (5:1–11 and possibly John 21:1–15). Since Jesus is one with the Father (10:30), he decides who lives and dies every day—animals and humans included. Jesus let Lazarus die (11:1–16) only to resurrect him later (11:38–44). I think that Jesus let Lazarus, many fish, and numerous pigs die to show his power over death. Revelation 1:18 NAB quotes Jesus (1:1–5 NAB), stating that he holds the keys to death, which means he has control and authority over everyone's mortality. On the contrary, humans do not have that power. Since Jesus has power over death, perhaps he made it so that the fish did not experience pain or suffering when they were caught with his help. Similarly, maybe he made it so that the demon-possessed pigs were shielded from agony. Although, Jesus did not protect Lazarus from illness (John 11:1–4), and presumably the suffering that went along with that before Lazarus died (11:11–21). Lazarus's illness happened because it brought glory to God the Father and Jesus (11:1–4). Jesus resurrected Lazarus (11:38–44), and there is good evidence that Jesus will do the same with the pigs and fish (and all animals for that matter) on the new earth (Ps 36:6; Luke 3:6).[48] Death will be the last enemy destroyed (1 Cor 15:26). On the new earth, God will destroy death forever (Rev 21:1–4 NLT) for all species (Rom 8:18–23 NLT). The harmonious and peaceful world of the new earth (Isa 11:6–9) will be full of an awareness of God's glory (Hab 2:14 NLT). Thus, whatever Jesus did to animals, no matter how grievous, should not upset us. Jesus knows the ultimate destiny of every creature (John 21:17). Additionally, Jesus (10:30) owns the animals and gave them life in the first place (Ps 104:24).

48. King, *I Will Abolish the Bow*, 79.

Additionally, I want to touch a little more on the Exorcism of the Gerasene Demoniac, where Jesus permitted multiple demons to possess around two thousand pigs, with the pigs eventually drowning (Matt 8:28–34; Mark 5:1–20; Luke 8:26–39). Jesus may have let this event occur to demonstrate authority over demons. For instance, in Luke 4:31–37, Jesus exorcised a demon from a man by simply demanding the demon to be silent and come out. It was said that Jesus had power and authority over unclean spirits. This exorcism caused reports about Jesus to spread to surrounding communities, which probably brought glory to Christ. Similarly, Lazarus's illness happened because it brought glory to God the Father and Jesus (John 11:1–4). Also, in John 9:1–2, the disciples asked Jesus why a man was born blind. In John 9:3, Jesus said, "It was not that this man sinned, or his parents, but that the works of God might be displayed in him." Jesus then made the man capable of seeing for the first time (9:6–7). Thus, perhaps the numerous pigs died (Mark 5:13) to ultimately show the work and glory of God, as the demons were exorcised (Matt 8:31–32) from two men (8:28). This exorcism caused the pig herdsman to flee into the city and tell what happened (8:33). The entire town then came out and met Jesus. Unfortunately, this event did not bring the (perhaps) intended glory of God, as the residents begged Jesus to leave the area (8:34). However, as I explained in *I Will Abolish the Bow*, I think the Exorcism of the Gerasene Demoniac (8:28–34; Mark 5:1–20; Luke 8:26–39) is best comprehended as an allegory[49]—especially if critics accuse the sinless Jesus (1 John 3:5 NLT) of animal cruelty (Prov 12:10 NLT). Regardless, Jesus' seemingly insensitive treatment of animals could be explained by timing.

When the Covenant Really Began

Perhaps Jesus did not show peace towards animals because the new covenant of Hos 2:18 may have not technically begun with his blood (Luke 22:20). There is considerable debate about when the new covenant (Heb 8:8–13) started. It is commonly thought that Jesus' blood-shedding death (John 19:30–34) initiated the new covenant (Matt 26:28 LSV). However, it is much more likely that the new covenant (1 Cor 11:25) started shortly after Pentecost (Acts 2:1) when the church became infused with the Holy Spirit (2:4). This timing of the new covenant can be most clearly seen when Peter (2:14) paraphrases Joel 2:28–32 (within Acts 2:16–21), which was prophetically fulfilled by the events seen at Pentecost (2:1–13).

49. King, *I Will Abolish the Bow*, 77.

Importantly, Peter (2:14) states, "in the last days" in Acts 2:17. Pentecost was nearly two thousand years ago, so this was not about the last days of this earth or the end times. I think that Peter (2:14) was describing the last days (2:17) of the old covenant (1 Sam 12:14-15). The book of Acts is dated between AD 80 and 130.[50] Additionally, Heb 8:13 states, "In speaking of a new covenant, he makes the first one obsolete. And what is becoming obsolete and growing old is ready to vanish away." The Epistle to the Hebrews is dated between AD 50 and 95.[51] Therefore, in Heb 8:13, we see that the old covenant was becoming obsolete but had not yet vanished. I interpret Acts 2:17 to be declaring that the old covenant (Exod 19:5) was in its last days, which means that it was probably close to ending. This timing would maybe explain why Jesus was seemingly insensitive to animals, as the new covenant of Hos 2:18 had not quite started yet. If the new covenant of Hos 2:18 began after Pentecost (Acts 2:1), Jesus had already ascended (1:6-11).

Before Pentecost (2:1), the church had about 120 people (1:15 CEV). The church included the original eleven apostles (1:13), Jesus' brothers and his mother (1:14), and the new twelfth apostle, Matthias, who was chosen to replace Judas (1:24-26). If the new covenant of Hos 2:18 started shortly after Pentecost (Acts 2:1), that would help explain the behavior of Christ's apostles. This timing would then explain why the apostles helped Jesus catch fish and then ate the fish (and bread) served by Jesus in John 21:1-15 (if John 21 was not a later addition). John 21:1-15 occurred before Pentecost (Acts 2:1). However, in *Demonstratio Evangelica* (Proof of the Gospels), Eusebius (c. AD 260-339) stated the apostles abstained from meat.[52] Perhaps the apostles abstained from meat only after Pentecost (2:1). Additionally, maybe the apostles passed on this meat-less tradition. This custom may explain why some early church fathers, including Saint Clement of Alexandria (c. AD 150-c. 215), Tertullian (c. AD 155-c. 220), Saint Basil the Great (AD 329-379), and Saint John Chrysostom (c. AD 347-407), were reportedly vegetarians. Additionally, the debatable early church father Origen of Alexandria (c. AD 185-c. 253) was ostensibly a vegetarian.[53] Again, the early church father Saint Jerome (c. AD 342-420) may have most significantly understood the Hos 2:18 new covenant as beginning before or

---

50. Kirby, "Book of Acts of the Apostles."
51. Kirby, "Book of Hebrews."
52. Bean, "Evidence That Jesus."
53. "Famous Vegetarians."

after Pentecost (Acts 2:1). He stated, "The consumption of animal flesh was unknown up until the great flood. But since the great flood, we have had animal flesh stuffed into our mouths. Jesus, the Christ, who appeared when the time was fulfilled, again joined the end to the beginning, so that we are now no longer allowed to eat animal flesh."[54]

Refutations

The reader may question my analysis of Jesus and his insensitivity to animals with several refutations. These refutations include the fact that the Bible tells Christians several times to imitate him and that Jesus never changes. The following paragraphs are an in-depth examination of these rebuttals to my claims.

Imitating Christ

Many Christians would counter my previous point—that it does not matter how Jesus behaved towards animals because of his divinity—by stating that the Bible tells Christians several times to imitate Jesus (John 13:15; Phil 2:5 NLT; 1 Pet 2:21; 1 John 2:6 NLT). If Christians are to imitate Jesus, doesn't this mean we should harm animals just like him? However, the contexts of John 13:15 (13:3–14, 16) and Phil 2:5 NLT (2:3–4 NLT, 2:6–8 NLT) are about Jesus humbling himself and becoming a servant.[55] Additionally, the context of 1 Pet 2:21 is about how God is pleased when Christians (1:1 NLT) patiently endure unfair treatment while doing God's will (2:19 NLT). Similarly, God is pleased when Christians patiently tolerate distress for doing good (2:20 NLT). Finally, there is the context of 1 John 2:6 NLT. First John 2:1–5 NLT indicates that observing Jesus' commandments shows that a Christian imitates him. Jesus' commandments include loving God (Matt 22:37–38), loving one another (John 13:34; 15:12, 15:17), honoring your parents, and loving your neighbor as yourself (Matt 19:19). Jesus' commandments also include the golden rule (7:12; Luke 6:31), be perfect (Matt 5:48), repent (4:17), pray for your persecutors and love your enemies (5:44), and forgive (18:21–22), as well as many others. Importantly, none of Jesus' commandments involve

54. Bean, "Evidence That Jesus."
55. King, *I Will Abolish the Bow*, 19.

harming animals. Actually, refraining from harming animals aligns with the golden rule, loving your neighbor as yourself, and servanthood.[56]

Hebrews 13:8

One objection to Jesus being vegan or being kind to animals today, even though he was not in biblical times, is Heb 13:8. This verse states, "Jesus Christ is the same yesterday and today and forever." This verse is employed to show that Jesus would make the same decisions today that he did about two thousand years ago. Thus, it is argued that Jesus would eat fish meat today as he (possibly) did then (Luke 24:41–43 NKJV). Based on Heb 13:8, it could be argued that Jesus would feed others fish flesh today as he (possibly) did then (Matt 14:13–21, 15:32–39; Mark 6:30–44, 8:1–10; Luke 9:10–17; John 6:1–15, 21:1–15). Based on Heb 13:8, it could be argued that Jesus would allow pigs to be demon-possessed and drowned today as he (possibly) did then (Matt 8:28–34; Mark 5:1–20; Luke 8:26–39). Finally, based on Heb 13:8, it could be stated that Jesus would help humans catch fish today as he did then (Luke 5:1–11; possibly John 21:1–15). However, the context of Heb 13:8 is essential. Hebrews 13:7 GNT indicates that the former leaders who spoke the message of God to Jewish believers (13:22 NLT) had died. I think God's message was best expressed by Acts 15:11, which states, "But we believe that we will be saved through the grace of the Lord Jesus, just as they will." I think that Heb 13:8 means that grace through Jesus (John 1:17) is permanent and perpetual, as the next verse (Heb 13:9) says it is good for the (believer's) heart to be strengthened by grace. Hebrews 13:9 also commands believers not to be led away by strange and diverse teachings, specifically about foods. Hebrews 13:7–9 GNT then communicates that Christians should remember their deceased leaders, who gave them God's message of grace through Jesus. This message never changes. Therefore, Christians should imitate their late leaders' faith and not be led away from the message by non-biblical teachings—specifically about obeying food rules. Thus, Heb 13:8 means that grace through Jesus never changes.

Regardless, based on the Bible, applying Heb 13:8 to Jesus' actions towards animals would not make sense because his behavior is implied to change in the future. For example, even though Jesus may have eaten fish meat in Luke 24:41–43 NKJV, when he returns (Matt 24:30), he is bringing

---

56. King, *I Will Abolish the Bow*, 18–20.

worldwide veganism with him. This veganism is implied by the description that no animals (or humans) will be harmed or killed (Isa 11:6–9; 65:25) on the eternal new earth (65:17–18). Thus, Jesus (John 10:30) is implied to be a vegan (like all of his believers) on the new earth (Rev 21:1–4 CEV). Additionally, saying that Jesus would act the same based on Heb 13:8 is dubious because his environment and circumstances would change throughout history. Thus, Heb 13:8 does not necessarily mean that he would act the same way if circumstances differed from biblical times. For example, it amazes me that Jesus never explicitly condemned slavery in the Bible. Although, it remains possible that he did, but it was never recorded. Regardless, most Christians today would agree that Jesus' silence over slavery in the Bible does not mean he would be silent against American slavery. The latter enslaved and tortured countless Africans and their descendants for generations. Biblical slavery, whether Hebrew or Roman, was not the same as United States race-based slavery.[57] Similarly, factory farming today is much different from how animals were farmed in biblical times. I am confident that Jesus would have some highly critical things to say about factory farming and the world's total meat consumption.

What Jesus ate when he walked the earth would also require an in-depth examination of the kosher restrictions (Lev 11:1–47; Deut 14:1–21). Jesus probably would have followed the kosher laws throughout his life on earth (2 Cor 5:21 NLT). Should Christians obey the kosher restrictions? With the new covenant of Hos 2:18 starting with the blood of Jesus (Luke 22:20) or after Pentecost (Acts 2:1), the kosher laws may have carried over from the Old Testament. It is traditionally understood that the kosher laws were put in place to make meat-eating more difficult for the Israelites. By putting restrictions on meat, God would make it more likely for the Israelites to live by the vegan ideal of Eden (Gen 1:26—2:8). Thus, the kosher restrictions would assist with achieving the new covenant of Hos 2:18. The next chapter focuses on kosher dietary laws—Lev 11:1–47 and Deut 14:1–21—and their applicability to the Christian.

---

57. King, *I Will Abolish the Bow*, 53.

7

Recognizing More Regulations

IN THE GARDEN OF Eden (Gen 2:15), God designed humans to be free
(1:26–27). However, after the fall (3:1–6), God allowed slavery (Lev
25:44–46) because humanity could not live up to (Exod 7:13–14) God's
Edenic (Gen 2:8) ideal of freedom (1:26–27). Thus, slavery was allowed but
restricted (Exod 21:26).[1] Therefore, if something is regulated in the Bible,
it tends to be not inherently good. Reverend Mathew Anderson stated it
this way,

> In giving laws to regulate slavery, God is not saying it is a good
> thing. In fact, by giving laws about it at all, He is plainly stating it
> is a bad thing. We don't make laws to limit or regulate good things.
> After all, you won't find laws that tell us it is wrong to be too healthy
> or that if water is too clean we have to add pollution to it. Therefore,
> the fact slavery is included in the regulations of the Old Testament
> at all assumes that it is a bad thing which needs regulation to pre-
> vent the damage from being too great.[2]

Following the pattern, in the beginning (Gen 1:1), God created (2:8)
the garden of Eden (2:15), where humans and animals only ate plants
(1:20–30, 2:7–25). God called this vegan paradise "very good" (1:31).
However, after the fall (3:1–6), eating animal flesh was permitted but given
restriction (9:3–4), which indicates that meat is not inherently good. Fittingly, one writer stated, "This startling warning underlines the fact that
eating flesh is not part of God's original intentions for creation. Indeed, it is

---

1. King, *I Will Abolish the Bow*, 53–54.
2. Hodge and Taylor, "Doesn't the Bible Support Slavery?," para. 26.

one of a number of regretful activities (e.g., the keeping of slaves, permission for the Israelites to take women in war, capital punishment, etc) which Jesus referred to as 'not so in the beginning' (Matthew 19:8), that is to say, permitted but only because of 'our hardness of heart.'"[3] However, before I continue, there is a difference in the Bible between "consecrated" meat and "secular" meat.

Consecrated Meat

The first consecrated meat may have been allowed to be eaten (Gen 9:3–4) after the clean animal sacrifices in Gen 8:20 to satisfy humanity's heart of evil intention (8:21). The consecrated meat prepared in Lev 6 and 7 was to be eaten after animals were sacrificed to temporarily (Heb 10:11 NLT) atone for human sin (Lev 6:1–7). An animal was killed and sacrificed for the burnt (6:9), sin (6:25), guilt (7:2), peace (7:11), vow, freewill (7:16), and wave (7:30) offerings. Depending on the offering type, the dead animal's flesh was required or permitted to be eaten by the priest(s) (6:26, 7:30–35), the offerer (7:15–16), or the males in the priest's family (6:28–29 NLT, 7:6 NLT). Eating consecrated meat was regulated with kosher laws (11:1–47; Deut 14:1–21) and anti-animal cruelty stipulations (Prov 12:10 NLT). Regarding the peace offerings, consecrated meat that touched something ceremonially unclean was required to be incinerated and not eaten. Only ceremonially clean people were allowed to eat consecrated meat from the peace offerings (Lev 7:19–21 NLT). Importantly, consecrated meat was strictly regulated, and only specific animal species were sacrificially appropriate. These individual animals required no blemishes or defects (Deut 17:1). The slaughter/sacrifice had to be done only in the religious centers in the cities of Jerusalem, Shiloh (1 Sam 1:3), and Mizpah. The flesh was consumed, but the blood (Lev 6:30, 7:26–27) and the fat (7:22–25) were not to be eaten. Furthermore, this consecrated meat was boiled (6:28 NLT). The boiling made the meat unpalatably mushy and unappetizing. Interestingly, the sons of Eli were called "worthless" because they wanted the consecrated flesh roasted instead of boiled, which angered God. The Almighty found Eli's sons disrespectful and guilty of sin (1 Sam 2:12–17). The boiled meat being unappetizing was to help regard animal sacrifice as an atoning action (Lev 6:1–7), not a reason for a cookout.[4] Maybe consecrated meat was

3. "But Didn't Jesus Eat Meat?," para. 8.
4. "But Didn't Jesus Eat Meat?," para. 9.

permitted (6:28–29 NLT) or required to be eaten (6:25–26) so that the sacrificial meat would not be wasted (John 6:11–12). Although, the primary reason for animal sacrifice was temporary (Heb 10:3–4) atonement for sin (Lev 6:1–7). Additionally, perhaps the sacrificial system (Gen 8:20) was fostered to obtain meat to eat (9:3–4) for humanity's heart of evil intention (8:21). Regardless, another type of consecrated meat was the lamb flesh that was required to be eaten yearly at Passover after the animal was killed/sacrificed (Exod 12:1–28).

Most importantly, animal sacrifice for the intention of temporary (Heb 10:11 NLT) sin atonement (Lev 6:1–7) ended when Jesus sacrificed himself instead (Heb 10:10–18 NLT). Thus, Jesus' sacrificial death (Mark 15:39 CEV) permanently (Heb 7:27 CEV) atoned for all human sin (1 John 2:1–2 NLT). Furthermore, eating the consecrated meat obtained from animal sacrifices—specifically Lev 6:24–30 NLT, 7:1–6 NLT, 7:11–21 NLT, and 7:28–36 NLT—was ended (Heb 10:10–18 NLT) and replaced by eating bread that represents the flesh of Christ (John 6:53–58). Similarly, the required annual Passover lamb sacrifice (Exod 12:1–28) was fulfilled when Jesus was sacrificed instead (1 Cor 5:7). As a result, Jesus symbolically (John 1:29, 1:36; 1 Pet 1:19 NLT) became the Passover lamb (1 Cor 5:7).[5] Additionally, the required annual Passover lamb sacrifice (Exod 12:1–28) was replaced with the Lord's Supper (Luke 22:17–20).[6] Finally, the annual requirement to eat the Passover lamb flesh (Exod 12:1–28) was fulfilled (1 Cor 5:7) and replaced with eating bread that symbolically represents the body (flesh) of Christ (Matt 26:26). In conclusion, animal sacrifice is no longer necessary because of the sacrifice of Jesus (Heb 10:10–18 NLT).[7] Thus, consecrated meat, which was obtained from animal sacrifices—specifically Lev 6:24–30 NLT, 7:1–6 NLT, 7:11–21 NLT, and 7:28–36 NLT—and killing the required annual Passover lamb (Exod 12:1–28), is no longer applicable to Christians today. Additionally, the permitted consecrated meat (Gen 9:3–4) obtained from animal sacrifices (8:20), as part of the "everlasting covenant" of Gen 8:20—9:17 was made null and void by Isa 24:5. However, secular meat remains on the menu.

5. King, *I Will Abolish the Bow*, 65.
6. King, *I Will Abolish the Bow*, 81.
7. King, *I Will Abolish the Bow*, 72.

Secular Meat

Secular meat is obtained by killing animals outside of the sacrificial procedures. The Hebrew of Deut 12 links secular meat with rebellion against God, wickedness, malefaction, lust, and as the result of the fall (Gen 3:1–6).[8] In the Old Testament, eating secular meat (Deut 12:15, 20–22) was similarly regulated with the kosher laws (Lev 11:1–47; Deut 14:1–21), anti-animal cruelty stipulations (Prov 12:10 NLT), and restriction from eating blood (Deut 12:16, 23–25). Additionally, eating secular meat was regulated with a gluttony restriction (Num 11:4–34 NLT; Prov 23:20–21). However, this same gluttony restriction did not apply to eating consecrated meat obtained from animal sacrifices (Gen 8:20—9:4; Lev 7:1–6 NLT, 7:11–21 NLT; Deut 12:17–19) or the required annual Passover lamb sacrifice (Exod 12:1–28). Traditionally, it is taught that there is continuity between the Old Testament (OT) and New Testaments (NT). Therefore, traditionally, it is taught that the OT moral law is still binding on Christians unless stated (or interpreted) otherwise in the NT. Importantly, if an OT moral law is repeated in the New Testament, it is definitely still required of Christians.

In *I Will Abolish the Bow*, I discussed two moral laws about eating secular meat still obligatory for Christians. The first is the eating of secular meat only when necessary for survival (the gluttony restriction), as seen in the Tale of the Desert Quail (Num 11:4–34 NLT) and Prov 23:20–21.[9] The Tale of the Desert Quail is retold in Pss 78:17–31 and 106:13–15. This gluttony restriction was also repeated in the New Testament. Christian meat-eaters love to quote 1 Cor 10:25 out of context. This verse states, "Eat whatever is sold in the meat market without raising any question on the ground of conscience." In context, this verse is talking about eating secular meat (10:27) from animals that had been sacrificed (10:18, 28) to idols (10:7, 14, 19) like demons (10:20–21). Importantly, at the beginning of the chapter (10:3–5 NLT), Paul and Sosthenes (1:1) summarize the Tale of the Desert Quail (Num 11:4–34 NLT). They then state the desert event occurred as a warning so that believers "would not crave evil things" like the foreigners and Israelites (11:4 NLT) did (1 Cor 10:6 NLT).

Thus, Paul and Sosthenes (1:1) imply that secular meat (Num 11:4 NLT, 11:34 NLT) is something evil (1 Cor 10:6 NLT). This association is not surprising, as God allowed meat consumption (Gen 9:1–4) only after

---

8. "But Didn't Jesus Eat Meat?," para. 10.

9. King, *I Will Abolish the Bow*, 56–58.

associating the human heart with evil intention (8:21). With 1 Cor 10:3–6 NLT, Paul and Sosthenes (1:1) were making clear that eating (10:27) the secular meat (10:25) obtained from a possible animal sacrifice to idols/demons (10:14–21) was ultimately regulated by the gluttony restriction (Num 11:4–34 NLT). Therefore, the Corinthians (1 Cor 1:2) could eat the possible idol/demon-sacrificed secular meat (10:14–27), but it must be necessary (10:3–6 NLT). Otherwise, they could end up like the desert quail-eaters of Num 11:4–34 NLT. Additionally, the Corinthians (1 Cor 1:2) were told to abstain from eating secular meat (10:25) if it was definitively used in idol/demon (10:14–21) sacrifice out of consideration for another's conscience (10:28–29). Importantly, this moral law restricting the gluttonous eating of meat (Num 11:4–34 NLT) is repeated in the New Testament (1 Cor 10:3–6 NLT) and is therefore still required to be followed by Christians. In *I Will Abolish the Bow*, I also discussed a second moral law regarding eating secular meat. This still binding moral law on Christians is Prov 12:10 NLT, which rebukes animal cruelty.[10] Thus, Christians must be sure that secular meat is essential and not removed from an animal treated cruelly. Additionally, other restrictions may be placed upon eating meat for Christians that need careful examination, namely the kosher dietary restrictions of Lev 11:1–47 and Deut 14:1–21.

Examining the Kosher Restrictions

The kosher dietary restrictions of Lev 11:1–47 and Deut 14:1–21 continue the theme of biblical slavery mentioned at the beginning of the chapter. The theme is that biblical restrictions assume that the action being restricted is a bad thing that needs regulation to inhibit excess harm. The Bible does not give a specific reason why the kosher dietary restrictions of Lev 11:1–47 and Deut 14:1–21 were put in place. Looking at the Bible comprehensively, I think the complicated kosher restrictions were intended to make obtaining meat more difficult by restricting permitted animal species. This difficulty would then push believers towards the vegan ideal (Gen 1:29) seen in Eden (2:8). Rabbi Shlomo Riskin thought similarly, stating, "The dietary laws were designed to teach us compassion and lead us gently back to vegetarianism."[11] Likewise, the greatly respected Rabbi Abraham Isaac Kook (AD 1865–1935) thought that the kosher restrictions were intended

10. King, *I Will Abolish the Bow*, 58.
11. Schwartz, "Letters to the Editor," para. 1.

to revere life while also attempting to discourage meat by making obstacles to its consumption.[12] Notably, I always thought that the kosher laws of Lev 11:1–47 and Deut 14:1–21 were no longer required of Christians. In multiple passages, the kosher restrictions were seemingly repealed in the New Testament. However, alternate interpretations exist for all of these NT passages. Thus, the kosher laws may still be binding on Christians. Therefore, I want to look at all the NT interpretations regarding the possible repeal of the kosher laws and see if they hold up to scrutiny. The most well-known NT kosher repeal interpretation is Peter's Vision of a Sheet with Animals in Acts 10:9–16 and 11:4–10.

Peter's Vision of a Sheet with Animals

In *I Will Abolish the Bow*, I interpreted the pericope known as Peter's Vision of a Sheet with Animals in Acts 10:9–16 as rescinding the kosher restrictions (Lev 11:1–47; Deut 14:1–21). I suspected this because Peter is told in Acts 10:13 to rise, kill, and eat.[13] This interpretation could be a broader application as Acts 10:14–15 talks about unclean and clean, respectively. However, that traditional interpretation seems to be taking this passage out of context, as a deeper inspection reveals that this is talking about calling certain humans common or unclean. Peter gives an interpretation of the pericope in Acts 10:17–33. Acts 10:28 holds the key, as Peter states, "You yourselves know how unlawful it is for a Jew to associate with or to visit anyone of another nation, but God has shown me that I should not call any person common or unclean." No verse in the Bible indicates gentiles are unclean. However, Judaism of that time made it unlawful for Jews to enter the homes of or even associate with gentiles, which supported the idea that gentiles were unclean.[14] Thus, Peter's Vision of a Sheet with Animals (10:9–16), declares that God deems no human as common or unclean (10:28). Peter repeated this point again in Acts 10:34–35, declaring that God accepts any human despite their nationality as long as they do right and fear God.

Further confirming this, Peter's Vision of a Sheet with Animals (10:9–16) is virtually retold in Acts 11:4–10. Again, in *I Will Abolish the Bow*, I interpreted Acts 11:4–10 as rescinding the kosher restrictions (Lev 11:1–47;

---

12. Schwartz, "Jewish Dietary Laws."

13. King, *I Will Abolish the Bow*, 65.

14. Aaron, "Acts 10."

Deut 14:1–21).[15] That traditional interpretation could be a broader application. However, the context clarifies that this is about Jews associating with
"unclean" humans. Acts 11:2–3 NLT says that Jewish believers scolded
Peter for eating with and entering the habitations of gentiles. Peter then re-
tells his vision of a sheet with animals in Acts 11:4–10, which was virtually
the same as Acts 10:9–16. Importantly, Acts 11:11–12 records Peter stating
(11:4), "And behold, at that very moment three men arrived at the house
in which we were, sent to me from Caesarea. And the Spirit told me to go
with them, making no distinction. These six brothers also accompanied
me, and we entered the man's house." Acts 11:11–12 NLT states that these
men sent from Caesarea were gentiles. Peter's vision in Acts 11:4–10 shows
that the Jewish believers who rebuked Peter for associating with gentiles
(11:2–3 NLT) were wrong. Thus, Peter's Vision of a Sheet with Animals in
Acts 11:4–10 also discusses unclean humans, which is not something that
exists in the eyes of God (11:11–12, 17–18). Although Peter's vision could
be broadly interpreted as a repeal of the kosher restrictions (Lev 11:1–47;
Deut 14:1–21), I find this unlikely. Again, the *Clementine Homilies* and the
Recognitions of Clement imply that Peter abstained from meat. This abstinence from meat would help explain why Peter stated in Acts 10:14, "By no
means, Lord; for I have never eaten anything that is common or unclean."
Peter said (11:4) something similar in Acts 11:8. Again, Peter stated in the
Clementine Homilies that consuming meat makes one associate with devils![16]
Thus, Peter declaring that his vision had something to do with making it
easier to eat meat by abrogating the kosher restrictions (Lev 11:1–47; Deut
14:1–21) would not fit his personal views.

Romans 14:14–20

In *I Will Abolish the Bow*, I discussed how Rom 14:14–20 seemed to nullify
the kosher restrictions of Lev 11:1–47 and Deut 14:1–21.[17] These kosher
laws discuss eating or not eating clean and unclean animals, respectively.
An alternate reading of Rom 14:14–20 is that Paul (1:1) was talking about
a different type of unclean. The word "unclean" has different biblical definitions—one being unclean animals, which are creatures restricted from
being eaten (Lev 11:1–47; Deut 14:1–21). Another biblical definition of

15. King, *I Will Abolish the Bow*, 65.
16. Bean, "Evidence That Jesus."
17. King, *I Will Abolish the Bow*, 65–66.

"unclean" is ceremonial uncleanness (like an association with idols in Ezek 36:25). The Greek word for unclean animals is *akatharton*. One of the Greek words for ceremonially unclean is the word *koinon*. Peter distinguished the two terms in Acts 10:14, stating, "By no means, Lord; for I have never eaten anything that is common [*koinon*] or unclean [*akatharton*]."[18] The two terms were distinguished almost identically in Acts 11:8. Peter (11:7) stated, "By no means, Lord; for nothing common [*koinon*] or unclean [*akatharton*] has ever entered my mouth."

In Rom 14:14, Paul (1:1) states, "I know and am persuaded in the Lord Jesus that nothing is unclean in itself, but it is unclean for anyone who thinks it unclean." In Rom 14:14, Paul (1:1) uses unclean (*koinon*) three times, obviously referring to ceremonial uncleanness. Romans 14:20 then states, "Do not, for the sake of food, destroy the work of God. Everything is indeed clean, but it is wrong for anyone to make another stumble by what he eats." The word "clean" in Rom 14:20 is translated from the Greek word *kathara*. In other verses of the Bible, *kathara* refers to the cleanliness of many types, including a sheet of linen fabric (Matt 27:59 NLT) and religion (Jas 1:27 DRB), but never meat from unclean animals.[19] The context of Rom 14 is about whether to consume meat from animals that were sacrificed to idols (14:1–3), which is made clearer in 1 Cor 8:1–13.[20] Based on the Hebrew text known as the *Mishna* (not the Bible), devout Jews believed foods sacrificed to idols were unclean.[21] In Rom 14:14–20, Paul (1:1) is most likely talking about how *biblically clean* (Lev 11:1–47; Deut 14:1–21) meat (Rom 14:1–3, 14:21) is not made (ceremonially) unclean if sacrificed to an idol, refuting the claim of the *Mishna*. Thus, in Rom 14:14–20, Paul (1:1) discusses the irrelevance of ceremonial uncleanness (Ezek 36:25) regarding food. Importantly, this irrelevance does not repeal the biblical kosher restrictions of not eating the flesh of unclean animals (Lev 11:1–47; Deut 14:1–21). Another common refutation to the kosher laws being in effect for Christians is Jesus seemingly declaring all foods clean in Mark 7:18–20.

18. Gitamondoc, "Answer to an Adventist," para. 15–18.
19. Gitamondoc, "Answer to an Adventist."
20. King, *I Will Abolish the Bow*, 91–92.
21. "Why Were Foods Offered," para. 2.

Jesus Declared All Foods Clean?

Mark 7:14–15 quotes Jesus as stating that nothing can go into someone and defile them, but rather the things that depart someone are what defiles them. Similarly, Mark 7:18–20 records Jesus as stating that food that enters the body cannot defile someone, but rather what exits a person defiles them, like evil things from the heart (7:21–23). Notably, Mark 7:19 parenthetically records the author's interpretation of Jesus proclaiming all foods clean. In *I Will Abolish the Bow*, I interpreted Mark 7:18–20 as Jesus rescinding the kosher restrictions of Lev 11:1–47 and Deut 14:1–21.[22] That traditional interpretation could be a broader application to Jesus' words. However, that traditional interpretation lifts Jesus' words out of context. The context indicates that unclean animals (*akatharton*) were not being discussed, but rather defiled (*koinais*) hands (Mark 7:2, 7:5). The difference in Greek words is significant. *Koinais* is a ceremonial impurity (uncleanness). Mark 7:6–13 sees Jesus rebuking the scribes and Pharisees (7:5). These groups were questioning Jesus as to why his disciples were eating with unwashed hands (7:1–2, 5). The Pharisees and scribes seemed to believe that eating with unwashed hands would make whatever food touched unclean, which would make the eater unclean upon ingestion. Mark 7:3 and 7:5 declare eating with washed hands as an elder tradition.

This handwashing tradition likely came from the *Mishna*. Someone might go into a market and touch ceremonially impure items. The *Mishna* said the impurity then had to be removed by washing all the way to the wrist.[23] It seems it was thought that unwashed hands could defile foods by touching them, which would defile the person upon ingestion.[24] This *Mishna* tradition may have been inspired by Exod 30:17–21, which required the priests (not the public) to wash their hands (and feet) for various sacred customs. Regardless, Jesus rightly affirmed this elder tradition as human-made, not a command from God (Mark 7:7–8, 7:13). Therefore, Mark 7:19's parenthetical declaration indicates that all foods are *ceremonially* clean, regardless of what the *Mishna* states. Alternatively, Mark 7:18–19's disputed portion is sometimes not even in parentheses depending on the translation (NKJV, ABPE, ISV, NHEB, WEB). Instead, these translations of Mark 7:18–19 seem to refer to the digestive tract purifying and/or expelling defiled foods.

22. King, *I Will Abolish the Bow*, 65.
23. Walker, "Surprise Sayings of Jesus Christ," para. 11.
24. Wheaton, "Did Yeshua Really Teach."

These translations would contextually align better, as Mark 7:18–23 NKJV, ABPE, ISV, NHEB, and WEB would mean that Jesus was basically saying that food cannot defile someone as it passes through digestion and excretion. Rather, it is the evil that comes from the heart that defiles a person. Regardless, numerous scholars theorize Mark 7:19's parenthetical interpretation of Jesus' words (7:18–19) may be a later addition. Bible scholar Geza Vermes thought that the Gospel editor inserted Mark 7:19's parenthetical interpretation and it did not originate from Jesus.[25] Nevertheless, the issue is made clearer in the Gospel of Matthew.

In Matt 15:10–11, Jesus similarly states that it is not what enters the mouth that defiles the individual but what exits the mouth that defiles them. Jesus later says that sins that depart the mouth from the heart are what defiles someone, not what they eat (15:16–19). Traditionally, these verses have been interpreted as Jesus repealing the kosher restrictions of Lev 11:1–47 and Deut 14:1–21. Indeed, in *I Will Abolish the Bow*, I interpreted Matt 15:16–18 to be about Jesus repealing kosher restrictions.[26] However, the context of Matt 15:1–9 records Jesus reprimanding the scribes and Pharisees, who had questioned why Jesus' disciples do not hand wash before they eat. Matthew 15:20 makes the issue clear, with Jesus stating about sins from the heart (15:19), "These are what defile a person. But to eat with unwashed hands does not defile anyone." Washing the hands before eating was an elder tradition (15:2), a human commanded (15:9) custom that was not from God (15:3, 6). Therefore, the issue of defilement relating to eating with unwashed hands was declared biblically non-authoritative (Mark 7:1–23; Matt 15:1–20), refuting the claims of the *Mishna*. Importantly, Mark 7:1–23 and Matt 15:1–20 do not repeal the biblical kosher restrictions pertaining to eating animals (Lev 11:1–47; Deut 14:1–21).

Additionally, in Luke 11:41, Jesus states, "But give as alms those things that are within, and behold, everything is clean for you." This verse would seem to repeal the kosher restrictions (Lev 11:1–47; Deut 14:1–21). However, in context, Jesus was attending a meal at a Pharisee's home. The host was surprised that Jesus did not wash his hands before the meal, as required by Jewish tradition (Luke 11:37–38 NLT). Jesus again implies this washing (and others) as a non-issue and states the Pharisees are wicked and greedy and can be cleaned of those sins by giving to the impoverished (11:39–41 NLT). Jesus reprimanded the Pharisees for being concerned about irrelevant

---

25. "Did 'Jesus' Say," para. 81–84.
26. King, *I Will Abolish the Bow*, 65.

outward cleanliness according to traditions (Mark 7:3–5), like cleansing their hands (Luke 11:37–38 NLT), dishes, and external cups (11:39). Jesus suggested that the Pharisees should be concerned about cleaning their internal filth (11:39–41 NLT) instead. Thus, in Luke 11:37–41 NLT, Jesus is rebuking the Pharisees for focusing on human-commanded (Mark 7:7) traditions (7:3–5) instead of God-prescribed righteous behavior (Prov 22:9 NLT). Importantly, Luke 11:37–41 does not repeal the biblical kosher restrictions pertaining to eating animals (Lev 11:1–47; Deut 14:1–21).

Finally, Titus 1:15 similarly states, "To the pure, all things are pure, but to the defiled and unbelieving, nothing is pure; but both their minds and their consciences are defiled." Some translations of Titus 1:15, like the DRB, ISV, and NAB, use "clean" instead of "pure." Therefore, Titus 1:15 could also be interpreted as a repeal of the kosher restrictions (Lev 11:1–47; Deut 14:1–21). However, the context states that the teachings (Titus 1:11 NIV) of truth rejecters, including Jewish myths and human commands, are to be ignored (1:14 NIV). These "Jewish myths" and "human commands" Paul (1:1) is referencing are probably human-commanded (Mark 7:7) Jewish traditions (7:3–4) that are not from God (7:8–9, 7:13). One such Jewish tradition is handwashing before eating (7:2–5). It would not make sense for Paul to label any books from the Bible as "myths," as he (Rom 1:1) implied the Old Testament to be the words of the Lord (3:2 NIV). Therefore, these "Jewish myths" and "human commands" (Titus 1:14 NIV) that mention cleanliness (1:15 NAB) cannot be about the kosher restrictions of Lev 11:1–47 and Deut 14:1–21. The kosher laws are from God (2 Tim 3:16 CEV). Another verse that seems to nullify the kosher restrictions is Col 2:16.

Colossians 2:16

In *I Will Abolish the Bow,* I interpreted Col 2:16 as repealing the kosher laws (Lev 11:1–47; Deut 14:1–21).[27] This abrogation is possible as a broad application, especially when reading Col 2:20–21. However, looking at the surrounding context, Col 2:22 CEV states, "After these things are used, they are no longer good for anything. So why be bothered with the rules that humans have made up?" Colossians 2:8 similarly states, "See to it that no one takes you captive by philosophy and empty deceit, according to human tradition, according to the elemental spirits of the world, and not according to Christ." Therefore, in Col 2:16, Paul and Timothy (1:1 NLT) are most

27. King, *I Will Abolish the Bow,* 94.

likely criticizing human-commanded (Mark 7:7) traditions (7:3–4) that are not from God (7:8–9, 13). These theologically irrelevant traditions may include eating with washed hands and washing cups, pots, copper containers, and furniture (7:2–5). Importantly, Col 2:16 does not repeal the God decreed laws of the kosher restrictions (Lev 11:1–47; Deut 14:1–21).

Though less convincing, an alternate interpretation of Col 2:16 notes the triple reference to a festival, a new moon, and the Sabbath. Colossians 2:16 may discuss the offerings of food and drink given during festivals, new moons, and Sabbaths. With Col 2:16, Paul and Timothy (1:1 NLT) may have been referencing, and thus repealing, Num 28:1—29:40 NIV, 1 Chr 23:31, 2 Chr 2:4, 8:12–13, 31:3, and Neh 10:33. These repealed passages/verses require, describe, or imply food (and drink) offerings to God on Sabbaths, new moons, and feast days/festivals.[28] In Col 2:16, Paul and Timothy (1:1 NLT) may declare that there is no longer any requirement to observe festivals/feast days, new moons, or Sabbaths, which was prophesied. Hosea 2:11 states, "And I will put an end to all her mirth, her feasts, her new moons, her Sabbaths, and all her appointed feasts." Therefore, Hos 2:11 was fulfilled with Col 2:16. In Rom 14:5–6, Paul (1:1 NLT) similarly states, "One person esteems one day as better than another, while another esteems all days alike. Each one should be fully convinced in his own mind. The one who observes the day, observes it in honor of the Lord. The one who eats, eats in honor of the Lord, since he gives thanks to God, while the one who abstains, abstains in honor of the Lord and gives thanks to God." However, the context of Rom 14:5–6 is about consuming meat from animals that were sacrificed to idols (14:1–3; 1 Cor 8:1–13).[29]

Since it may no longer be required to observe any festival, new moon, or Sabbath, Col 2:16 would declare that the food and drink offerings on those special days are no longer obligatory either. This declaration is because of the sacrifice of Jesus (Heb 10:12–18 NLT). Jesus fulfilled these offerings, broadly replacing the food and drink offerings with his body and blood, which was symbolized with bread and wine, respectively (Matt 26:26–29). This replacement was part of the new covenant (Luke 22:17–20). Notably, Jesus stated in John 6:55, "For my flesh is true food, and my blood is true drink." Thus, Col 2:16 may be repealing food and drink requirements in specific circumstances like festivals, new moons, or Sabbaths. Therefore, Col 2:16 is probably not repealing the kosher restrictions (Lev 11:1–47;

28. Papaioannou and Sokupa, "Does Colossians 2:16, 17 Abolish."
29. King, *I Will Abolish the Bow*, 91–92.

Deut 14:1–21). Unfortunately, many Christians take Col 2:16 and run with it as far as possible, even applying it to moral issues regarding food, like animal cruelty (Prov 12:10 NLT). I have seen Christians quote Col 2:16 to justify even meat from factory farmed animals. However, no Christian scholar would say that every form of food (and drink) is acceptable with Col 2:16. For instance, if one went to a party hosted by someone like Hannibal Lecter, I doubt they would find a human corpse prepared for consumption acceptable based on Col 2:16. That would violate the command not to murder (Exod 20:13)!

Colossians 2:16 seems to have rescinded food and drink offering requirements for festivals/feast days, new moons, and Sabbaths. Colossians 2:16 appears to have also repealed the obligation to observe those special days. How then should one understand Ezek 45:17? This verse states, "It shall be the prince's duty to furnish the burnt offerings, grain offerings, and drink offerings, at the feasts, the new moons, and the Sabbaths, all the appointed feasts of the house of Israel: he shall provide the sin offerings, grain offerings, burnt offerings, and peace offerings, to make atonement on behalf of the house of Israel." Ezekiel 45:17 is part of a section that prophesies a future temple (40–48) featuring a seeming return to food/drink offerings, animal sacrifices, and celebrating festivals/feast days, new moons, and Sabbaths. However, I discussed in *I Will Abolish the Bow* how Christ symbolically became (1 Cor 15:3–4) this prophesied (Ezek 40–48) temple (John 2:19–22; Rev 21:22).[30] Jesus specifically became the foretold (Isa 28:16) foundation (1 Cor 3:11 CEV) and cornerstone (Eph 2:20–22 NLT) of this spiritual temple (Mark 14:58). The prophets and the apostles and are also part of the foundation (Eph 2:20 NLT). Believers are individual stones built upon the cornerstone and foundation to become a spiritual temple (2:20–22 NLT). Believers are also holy priests who offer God-pleasing spiritual sacrifices (1 Pet 2:4–5 NLT) like praise to God (Heb 13:15).

Thus, Ezekiel's prophesied temple (Ezek 40–48) was spiritually realized (Mark 14:58) in Christ (John 2:19–22), the apostles, the prophets, and Jesus' followers (Eph 2:20–22 NLT; 1 Pet 2:4–5 NLT). The food/drink offerings (specifically Ezek 45:17) and animal sacrifices mentioned throughout Ezek 40–48 were fulfilled with spiritual sacrifices (1 Pet 2:4–5 NLT). Other biblical verses outside of Ezekiel that prophesy future animal sacrifices (and offerings), like Jer 33:18 NLT, Isa 56:6–7, and 60:6–7 CEV, were also realized with spiritual sacrifices from Christians (1 Pet 2:4–5 NLT). Additionally,

---

30. King, *I Will Abolish the Bow*, 73–74.

the priests mentioned throughout Ezek 40–48 and Jer 33:18 NLT—who will seemingly offer these future animal sacrifices (and offerings)—were realized in Christ's believers, who offer spiritual sacrifices (1 Pet 2:4–5 NLT) instead. Ezekiel 45:17 is also fulfilled in Col 2:16, which seems to repeal any requirement of observing Sabbaths, feast days/festivals, or new moons and the obligatory food and drink offerings on those special days. This fulfillment seems to be confirmed with Col 2:17. The verse states, "These are a shadow of the things to come, but the substance belongs to Christ." This verse shows that these special days and food/drink offerings of Col 2:16 were fulfilled in Jesus.

Hebrews 9:10 CEV is similar to Col 2:16 by addressing food and drink. Hebrews 9:10 CEV states, "These rules are merely about such things as eating and drinking and ceremonies for washing ourselves. And rules about physical things will last only until the time comes to change them for something better." This verse could be interpreted as repealing the kosher restrictions (Lev 11:1–47; Deut 14:1–21). However, in context, Heb 9:9 CEV mentions offering sacrifices and gifts. Therefore, Heb 9:9–10 CEV seems to be referencing the food and drinks (Num 29:36–37) that were offered in sacrifice for sins by the high priest (Heb 5:1).[31] Importantly, Jesus fulfilled these sacrifices, broadly replacing the food and drink offerings with his body and blood, which were symbolized with bread and wine, respectively (Matt 26:26–29). This replacement was part of the new covenant (Luke 22:17–20). Jesus stated in John 6:55, "For my flesh is true food, and my blood is true drink." Furthermore, based on the title and contents, the Hebrews Epistle was seemingly written to Jewish Christians. Most of these intended readers were probably born and raised under the Torah. Therefore, I think it probably would have been clear if the author was trying to repeal the kosher laws of Lev 11:1–47 and Deut 14:1–21. Most importantly, are the kosher restrictions still binding on Christians today?

The Kosher Law Conclusion

A strong case exists for kosher restrictions still being obligatory for Christians. Many church denominations believe this is the case. For instance, the Seventh-day Adventist (SDA) Church and United Church of God (UCG) typically expect members to follow the kosher restrictions of Lev 11:1–47 and Deut 14:1–21. The kosher restrictions still being applicable would

31. Papaioannou and Sokupa, "Does Colossians 2:16, 17 Abolish," para. 18.

make sense in the context of the new covenant of Hos 2:18. I think that the kosher laws of Lev 11:1–47 and Deut 14:1–21 still being required for Christians seem to depend on interpretation. It seems ambiguous enough where it could go either way. However, the kosher laws remaining binding for Christians would make sense as the notion that God is offended by humans who eat unclean meat, especially pig flesh, is consistent throughout Scripture (Isa 65:2–5 NASB; 66:17). Regardless, I do think that other dietary restrictions are indisputably applicable to Christians and still binding. These dietary restrictions are part of the Jerusalem Quadrilateral (Acts 15:19–20, 28–29, 21:25).

The Jerusalem Quadrilateral

Acts 15:1–21 describes an important event in the history of the early church, which is known as the Jerusalem Council. At this Council, Paul, Barnabas (15:2, 12), Peter (15:7), James (15:13), elders, apostles (15:6), Pharisee-influenced believers (15:5), and others (15:2) discussed (15:7) if circumcision was necessary for salvation (15:1). Some Pharisee-influenced believers wanted converted gentiles to be required to be circumcised and obligated to keep the laws of the Torah (15:5 NLT). The elders and apostles discussed the matter together. Peter (15:6–7) emphasized that salvation is achieved through the grace of Jesus (15:11). Thus, regardless of the outcome in Jerusalem (15:2), the issue was not over salvation. Peter (15:7) also implied that circumcision (15:1) and following the Torah laws (15:5) are a burden that the gentile believers should not bear because it was too difficult for the Jews of the present and past (15:10 NLT). Thus, the Council came to four requirements of gentile believers, which are specified in Acts 15:19–20 and are known as the "Jerusalem Quadrilateral." Acts 15:19–20 states, "Therefore my judgment is that we should not trouble those of the gentiles who turn to God, but should write to them to abstain from the things polluted by idols, and from sexual immorality, and from what has been strangled, and from blood." These four stipulations are essentially repeated in Acts 15:28–29 and 21:25. Acts 15:28 indicates that the Holy Spirit approved of these four requirements. Notably, the Jerusalem Quadrilateral (15:19–20, 28–29, 21:25) may be based on Lev 17:1—18:30. Importantly, the question is how the modern Christian should interact with these four stipulations.

Abstain from Sexual Immorality

There seems to be universal agreement that one of these requirements, abstaining from sexual immorality, is still binding on Christians, as it is part of the moral law (18:1–30). I agree that abstaining from sexual immorality is still binding on Christians, as it is repeated elsewhere in the New Testament (1 Thess 4:3). However, the other three stipulations within the Jerusalem Quadrilateral (Acts 15:19–20, 28–29; 21:25), which relate to food, have no consensus on what is required today. Many Christian scholars believe that these food laws were only related to that time to develop harmony between gentile and Jewish Christians. The issues of things polluted by idols (Lev 17:7), strangled animals (17:13), and abstaining from blood (17:10–14) were issues that the Christian Jews would be sensitive to due to their Old Testament knowledge. However, the inclusion of sexual immorality within the Jerusalem Quadrilateral (Acts 15:19–20, 28–29; 21:25) indicates that these were probably not temporary stipulations.[32] I think Christians need to look at other parts of the New Testament that make these issues clearer.

Abstain from Things Polluted by Idols

The most convoluted requirement is the issue of "things polluted by idols." The NLT and CEV of Acts 15:20, 15:29, and 21:25 clarify that this requirement is to avoid consuming food sacrificed to idols. Exodus 34:14–15 NLT; Num 25:2–3 NLT, Ps 106:28–29 NIV, Rev 2:14, and 2:20 criticize ingesting food sacrificed to idols. This idea is strengthened in 1 Cor 10:1–33 when Paul and Sosthenes (1:1) say to flee from idol worship (10:14), such as (food and drink) sacrifices to idols (demons) (10:19–21). However, (secular) meat from sacrificed animals sold at the market was allowed to be eaten (10:25–27). Yet, Christians (1:2) were to abstain from eating the flesh if someone's conscience was offended (10:32) by the sacrifice (10:28–29). This explanation may seem like a contradiction, but there is a distinction between time and place. Directly consuming foods sacrificed to idols during a worship event to said idols was sinful (Num 25:2–3 NLT). However, Paul and Sosthenes (1 Cor 1:1) state that secular meat obtained from animals that were offered to idols (demons) previously (10:19–21), but were then sold at a market, were not sinful to eat (10:25–27). However, the meat

---

32. Wayne, "Commands of Acts 15:20."

should be shunned if it offended (10:32) someone's conscience (10:28–29). Author Luke Wayne clarifies the issue well, stating,

> The issue is to avoid eating in a context in which the eating was, in fact, a form of worship to the idol. Thus, it is always wrong to join in an overtly idolatrous feast where eating is perceived as an act of worship. It is not objectively wrong, however, to eat common meat from the market that was sacrificed to an idol at some earlier time. If, however, one's conscience is bothered by this, you should abstain for the sake of conscience without binding your brother who does not share your concern. Likewise, you should not flaunt your freedom by eating something in front of a brother who may have stricter personal convictions on the matter than you do.[33]

It is important to remember that Paul and Sosthenes (1:1) regulated this meat-eating (10:25–27) at the beginning of the chapter (10:3–6 NLT) by referencing the gluttony restriction (Num 11:4–34 NLT). Earlier, in 1 Cor 8:1–13, Paul and Sosthenes (1:1) addressed the issue of consuming left-over (10:19–27) food sacrificed to idols. They imply that the topic of eating idol-offered food is trivial because idols are not real (8:4–6). However, they also implicate that Christians (1:2) must abstain if a fellow believer's weak conscience is wounded by witnessing them eat idol sacrificed food (8:7–12). Paul and Sosthenes (1:1) proclaim in 1 Cor 8:13, "Therefore, if food makes my brother stumble, I will never eat meat, lest I make my brother stumble." Similarly, in Rom 14:1–23, Paul (1:1) also addresses the issue of foods sacrificed to idols. He concludes the same, implying that eating leftover secular meat from idolatrous sacrifice (1 Cor 10:19–27) is inconsequential (Rom 14:1–6).[34] However, it is implied that Christians should abstain if other believers are offended by it (14:13–20). Notably, Paul (1:1) states in Rom 14:21, "It is good not to eat meat or drink wine or do anything that causes your brother to stumble." This issue is cited in both the Old (Exod 34:14–15 NLT; Num 25:2–3 NLT; Ps 106:28–29 NIV) and New (Rev 2:14, 20) Testaments, as well as the Jerusalem Quadrilateral (Acts 15:19–20 NLT/CEV, 15:28–29 NLT/CEV; 21:25 NLT/CEV). Thus, abstaining from consuming foods sacrificed to idols (at the worship ceremony only) is still binding on Christians. Regardless, this is not an issue that most Christians will ever have to contemplate today, except maybe if the meat was something like "halal certified."

33. Wayne, "Commands of Acts 15:20," para. 28.
34. King, *I Will Abolish the Bow*, 91–92.

Abstain from What Has Been Strangled and from Blood

The stipulation about abstaining from what was strangled seems somewhat related to the requirement to avoid blood. The NLT of Acts 15:19–20, 15:28–29, and 21:25 indicate the obligations are to abstain from consuming the flesh of strangled animals and avoid eating blood. Consuming blood (from meat) is condemned throughout Scripture (Gen 9:4; Lev 19:26; Deut 15:19–23). I think that eating blood is prohibited out of concern for hygiene since blood is known to transmit disease.[35] Avoiding the consumption of strangled animal flesh is less biblically clear. Garroting an animal is not considered a proper biblical way to slaughter an animal, as Lev 17:13 requires the edible creature to be exsanguinated. Theoretically, strangling the animal would not allow the dead animal to bleed out.[36] Therefore, eating meat from a strangled animal would lead to eating (coagulated) blood. Consequently, I think the stipulations of abstaining from consuming the flesh of strangled animals and avoiding eating blood are still required for Christians. Nothing specifically in the New Testament clarifies or nullifies them. Likewise, I believe the rule to avoid eating garroted animal flesh is still obligatory because it continues the moral law of Prov 12:10 NLT. This verse condemns animal cruelty. Strangling would probably be seen as a cruel way to kill an animal. Therefore, eating the flesh of a strangled animal would make one an accomplice in the cruelty.

The Jerusalem Quadrilateral Conclusion

The question over the kosher laws (Lev 11:1–47; Deut 14:1–21) being required for Christians is highly interpretable. In contrast, I think that Christians are (still) bound to the requirements of the Jerusalem Quadrilateral (Acts 15:19–20, 28–29, 21:25). This conclusion comes after careful study and acknowledging continuity regarding actions that God finds particularly reprehensible (Ezek 33:25–26). Indeed, like slavery, the biblical restrictions on meat-eating assume that it is something bad that needs to be regulated to mitigate the damages it causes. Importantly, the Jerusalem Quadrilateral restrictions (Acts 15:19–20, 28–29, 21:25) align with the new covenant of Hos 2:18, as the constraints would make meat-eating more difficult and veganism more encouraged.

35. King, *I Will Abolish the Bow*, 57.
36. "Strangled."

Summary of Meat Restrictions

In conclusion, the Christian Animal Rights Association teaches that eating secular meat has several restrictions that are binding on the Christian. These restrictions include the Jerusalem Quadrilateral (Acts 15:19–20, 15:28–29; 21:25), as well as the moral laws prohibiting cruelty to animals (Prov 12:10 NLT) and gluttony (Num 11:4–34 NLT; Pss 78:17–31; 106:13–15; Prov 23:20–21; 1 Cor 10:3–6 NLT). Additionally, because the kosher restrictions are intended to discourage meat procurement and eating, our ministry interprets following the kosher laws (Lev 11:1–47; Deut 14:1–21) as an obligation for Christians. Therefore, our ministry interprets the binding secular meat-eating restrictions as applying to *flesh sanctioned by the Bible*, which is only from clean animals (Lev 11:1–47; Deut 14:1–21). In conclusion, like slavery, all of these biblical restrictions on meat-eating assume that it is something bad that needs to be regulated to mitigate the damages it causes. All of these regulations align with the new covenant of Hos 2:18, as they make meat-eating difficult and thus encourage veganism. Based on Hos 2:18 NIV, the Christian Animal Rights Association encourages veganism. With these required regulations, the reader may have further questions. The next chapter focuses on common questions Christians may have about meat.

8

Questions about Meat

Is the Consumer Responsible for Animal Cruelty?

PROVERBS 12:10 NLT CONDEMNS cruelty to animals. Yet, modern animal agriculture is tremendously and almost always cruel, even by biblical standards. Worldwide, billions of animals are killed per year for food, who are usually ruthlessly confined and mercilessly killed with little regard for their pain and suffering. Their short, painful lives end in horrific and ghastly ways. The only time they see sunlight is typically on their way to the abattoir. Of course, they get no consideration upon transport either. Footage often shows these animals frozen to death or severely shivering during the winter. In the summer, some of these transported animals have been seen cooked alive or likely suffering from a heat stroke from the harsh scorching weather they are forced to endure. In summary, the meat, dairy, and egg industries are tremendously cruel in modern industrial agriculture today.

After showing or explaining this footage to Christians, a typical response is that they pay for the meat (and other animal products), not the cruelty. This cop-out is hardly excusable, but I will give it weight for a brief second. Are Christians responsible for animal cruelty if it is caused secondhand? Beyond the obvious yes, there is also Scripture to support this. Jesus stated to his disciples in Luke 17:1–2 (CEV), "There will always be something that causes people to sin. But anyone who causes them to sin is in for trouble. A person who causes even one of my little followers to sin would be better off thrown into the ocean with a heavy stone tied around their neck." Also, 1 Tim 5:22 says not to participate in others' sins.

Additionally, Eph 5:11 tells Christians (1:1) not to participate in unproductive works of darkness. So, what should Christians do instead? Ephesians 5:11 says to expose these unfruitful dark works. When applying this verse, the proper behavior for Christians is not to participate in eating meat (and other animal products). Instead, Christians should stop participating in the demand for meat (and other animal products) and expose the footage of what cruelty animals go through in modern industrial agriculture.

What About 1 Timothy 4:4-5?

In *I Will Abolish the Bow*, I discussed how 1 Tim 4:1-3 is commonly and inaccurately utilized to criticize vegetarians and vegans. I concluded that 1 Tim 4:1-3 condemns Gnosticism.[1] Importantly, 1 Tim 4:4-5 states, "For everything created by God is good, and nothing is to be rejected if it is received with thanksgiving, for it is made holy by the word of God and prayer." It could be interpreted that 1 Tim 4:4-5 repeals the kosher laws (Lev 11:1-47; Deut 14:1-21). However, there is no mention of "clean" or "unclean" anywhere in the context, so this is unlikely. In 1 Tim 4:4, Paul (1:1) seems to cite Gen 1:29-31, the passage where God tells all humans and animals only to eat the plants. Eating plant foods was called "very good" (1:29-31). Thus, when 1 Tim 4:4 says that "everything is good," that means only plant foods. The Greek word for meat is *krea* (Rom 14:21; 1 Cor 8:13), which is not used in 1 Tim 4:4-5 or the context. Importantly, in 1 Tim 4:3, Paul (1:1) uses the Greek word *brōmatōn*, a nonspecific word meaning food. This word choice, plus the seeming citation of Gen 1:29-31, indicates that meat was not being discussed in 1 Tim 4:1-8. Thus, regarding foods (4:3) in 1 Tim 4:1-8, Paul (1:1) only discusses edible vegetation.

With 1 Tim 4:4-5, Paul (1:1) was probably correcting the gnostics who believed that physical matter, like (plant) food, is evil and the work of a malevolent creator known as the "demiurge." In 1 Tim 4:7, Paul (1:1) calls these gnostic beliefs "irreverent, silly myths." In contrast, in 1 Tim 4:4-5, Paul (1:1) references how (plant) food (4:3) is a blessing from God, seemingly citing Gen 1:29-31. First Timothy 4:8 then describes "bodily training," which may be describing a strict form of food deprivation involving extreme calorie restriction, minimal food options, and persistent fasting. This strict food deprivation was intended to discipline one's body.[2] Thus,

---

1. King, *I Will Abolish the Bow*, 94.
2. Newall, "Bible and Veganism," 14-15.

1 Tim 4:1–8 seems to be criticizing Gnosticism, specifically their severe (plant) food deprivation and forbidding of marriage. A summary of 1 Tim 4:1–8 would be that Christians should avoid the teachings of the gnostics, who required severe (4:7–8) abstention from (plant) foods (and prohibit marriage) because of their false beliefs (4:1–3) that matter (including plant food) is evil. On the contrary, God proclaimed that all (plant) food is good, and thus Christians should not abstain from these (plant) foods if they are received by thanking God (4:4–5). These gnostic beliefs in severe (plant) food deprivation (4:8) and marriage prohibition (4:3–4) are disrespectful, foolish, and fictitious (4:7).

A big reason 1 Tim 4:4–5 is thought to discuss meat is inaccurate translations (BLB, KJB, NKJV, ASV, DRB, ERV, LSV, NHEB, WEB, YLT). These translations of 1 Tim 4:4 state that each *creature* is good instead of the ESV's "everything *created* by God is good." The NIV, NLT, NASB, AMP, CSB, HCSB, CEV, GNT, ISV, NAB, NRSV, and WNT have a similar (or identical) translation of 1 Tim 4:4 as the ESV. The confusion results from the translation of the Greek word, *ktisma,* which can be translated as the English "creatures," "created," or "created thing,"[3] depending on the context. For instance, most translations of Rev 5:13 properly render *ktisma* to "creature" as the verse seems to describe animals speaking (or singing) in various places. Looking at context, I think that *ktisma* in 1 Tim 4:4 is talking only about (created) plants as Paul (1:1) seems to reference only the vegetation as food (Gen 1:29–31), and 1 Tim 4:3 discusses foods.

Gnosticism may be criticized again in Heb 13:9, which states, "Do not be led away by diverse and strange teachings, for it is good for the heart to be strengthened by grace, not by foods, which have not benefited those devoted to them." Hebrews 13:10–16 GNT then references priests eating meat obtained from Jewish temple animal sacrifices. These lawful sacrifices were fulfilled in Jesus' death and replaced with spiritual sacrifices like helping one another, praising God, and doing good. Therefore, Heb 13:9 could be speaking about the kosher laws (Lev 11:1–47; Deut 14:1–21). However, Heb 13:9 is more likely criticizing Gnosticism, much like 1 Tim 4:1–8 does. Explicitly, Heb 13:9 GNT criticizes these ambiguous rules concerning foods, calling them strange and unhelpful. Similarly, 1 Tim 4:1–2 says the gnostic abstention from (plant) foods (4:3–8) are taught by demons through insincere liars. Another possibility is that Heb 13:9 criticizes human-made commands[4]

3. "Ktisma."
4. Link, "Would You Please Explain."

(Matt 15:9), like handwashing before eating (15:2 NIV)—much like Jesus did in Matt 15:3–20. This connection makes more sense. Why would Heb 13:9 GNT call the God instructed kosher restrictions (Lev 11:1–47; Deut 14:1–21) strange and unhelpful? The Epistle to the Hebrews was written to a Jewish Christian audience who most likely would not have found the kosher restrictions (Lev 11:1–47; Deut 14:1–21) to be strange. Therefore, Heb 13:9 is most likely criticizing Gnosticism (1 Tim 4:1–8) or human-made commands (Isa 29:13).

What about Hunting, Trapping, and Fishing?

Before I begin, I think that most of the verses or passages in the Bible about hunting, trapping, and fishing should be considered "descriptive," not "prescriptive." A descriptive passage or verse describes what happened or will happen and is not necessarily an endorsement of the behavior. A prescriptive passage or verse indicates that God commands or encourages the conduct. It is essential to recognize this theological distinction. I have debated many times with hunters, who usually quote-mine the Bible with Gen 27:3. The verse states, "Now then, take your weapons, your quiver and your bow, and go out to the field and hunt game for me." Many hunters think that God is commanding this. In context, this is Isaac telling his son Esau to go and hunt for him (27:1–3). Then, Gen 27:4 has Isaac stating to Esau, "and prepare for me delicious food, such as I love, and bring it to me so that I may eat, that my soul may bless you before I die." Esau complied and went hunting (27:5). Isaac's words to Esau (27:3–4) were paraphrased by Rebekah to Jacob (27:6) in Gen 27:7. Genesis 27:1–7 is merely a description of events, not a prescription from God. Looking closer, though, Esau was a hunter, and God did not like him. Esau was a skilled hunter, and his father Isaac loved him because of the carcasses he brought back to eat (25:27–28). Malachi 1:2–3 has God stating that he hated Esau, which is repeated in Rom 9:13. Hebrews 12:16 may indicate that God hated Esau because he was sexually immoral and unholy. Could it additionally be that God hated Esau because he was a hunter? First Samuel 26:20 NLT and Lam 3:52 negatively portray the hunting of birds (and thus, possibly all animals) through metaphor. Does Esau's callousness to God's desires (like moral sex and holiness) manifest in Esau's choice to hunt? I think so, considering that God states that the new covenant (Luke 22:20) results in the breaking of the bow (Hos 2:18 NHEB). God prefers that humanity would not hunt (Gen

1:26–31), which is why there is no hunting (Isa 11:6–9) on the eternal new earth (65:17–18).

Genesis 10:9 could be used to defend biblical hunting, as it states, "He was a mighty hunter before the LORD. Therefore it is said, 'Like Nimrod a mighty hunter before the LORD.'" Genesis 10:9's description of him seems to be just a description, not an endorsement from God. Genesis 10:8 and 1 Chr 1:10 both describe Nimrod as the son of Cush and the earth's first mighty man. Furthermore, Nimrod established the city of Babel (Gen 10:9–10). The tower and the city were built together (11:4–5). Thus, Nimrod would likely have helped construct the Tower of Babel (11:1–9). This conclusion is recognized in multiple Hebrew writings.[5] Importantly, the reader may be familiar with the insulting English slang of calling someone a "nimrod." The Merriam-Webster Dictionary defines the slang term as an "idiot" or a "jerk." The source states that the biblical Nimrod did not have a reputation as a compassionate leader. His name has been used to mean "tyrant." However, this meaning is now basically outdated. His name is also used to label "someone who is stupid." This label is derived from Nimrod's connection with the tower of Babel, which brought God's wrath.[6] Thus, there is evidence that Nimrod was not an exemplar of virtue, and his hunting is a further indication.

However, Gen 21:20 seems like God supports hunting, as it states, "And God was with the boy, and he grew up. He lived in the wilderness and became an expert with the bow." This verse speaks about Ishmael, the son of Hagar and Abraham (21:9 NLT). Ishmael admittedly does not fit my narrative of biblical figures that hunted and thus were frowned upon by God, as Ishmael was blessed by God (17:19–20). However, in context, Ishmael and his mother were sent away by Abraham into the Beersheba wilderness (21:14). Ishmael eventually resided in the Paran wilderness (21:21). I do not think this was God being happy with Ishmael's hunting, probably more just his tolerance of it as a necessity. Ishmael probably did not have many options for food when he was in the wild. However, Ishmael's behavior was not always pleasant. Abraham's wife Sarah (20:2) seemingly despised Ishmael, and she was behind why Abraham banished Ishmael and his mother. It seems that Sarah became angry at Ishmael for mocking her son Isaac (21:9–10 NASB). Following rabbinic biblical commentary, the French Rabbi Shlomo Yitzhaki, better known as "Rashi" (AD 1040–1105), connected

---

5. Roat, "7 Facts You Didn't Know," para. 23–25.

6. "Nimrod."

Ishmael with murder, idolatry, and unlawful sexual interactions. This connection would better clarify why Sarah seemingly despised Ishmael and demanded him to be sent away (21:9–10 NASB). Although, the commentary and Rashi's implication may be too severe.[7] Regardless, it turns out that Ishmael may not have been an admirable individual, which might explain why he hunted. Additionally, keep in mind that just because God blesses a biblical figure does not exactly mean that God supports everything that they do. For instance, Samson was blessed by God (Judg 13:24), but he later set fire—by cruelly using three hundred foxes—to the Philistines' crops (15:4–5) out of revenge (15:11). Yet, revenge is condemned in Prov 20:22 GNT. Additionally, animal cruelty is condemned in Prov 12:10 NLT. Similarly, just because God blessed Ishmael, it does not necessarily mean that God found his hunting acceptable. Thus, there seems to be a consistent biblical theme that hunting is associated with poor character.

Proverbs 12:27 states, "Whoever is slothful will not roast his game, but the diligent man will get precious wealth." This verse could be interpreted as a license to hunt. Importantly, Proverbs sometimes expresses a principle by using unpleasant imagery. I do not think Prov 12:27 is an endorsement of hunting. Instead, it communicates that a hardworking person will succeed while a lazy person will fail. This type of expression happens elsewhere in Proverbs. For instance, Prov 13:24 could be used to justify child abuse, stating, "Whoever spares the rod hates his son, but he who loves him is diligent to discipline him." However, minus the unpleasant imagery, the principle is that parental discipline of children is essential. Proverbs 13:24 CEV captures the focus of the verse, stating, "If you love your children, you will correct them; if you don't love them, you won't correct them." The principle of Prov 13:24 does not require corporal punishment to communicate the author's (seeming) intent. Therefore, it is crucial to decipher the essence of the proverb, not the extraneous details the writer uses to communicate it. Thus, I think that Prov 12:27 GNT captures the principle of the verse perfectly, stating that if one works hard, one will gain success. However, if one is lazy, one will not be successful. Therefore, Prov 12:27 has little to do with hunting.

Additionally, Isa 49:2 may conjure some hunting imagery with the mention of an arrow. The verse states, "He made my mouth like a sharp sword; in the shadow of his hand he hid me; he made me a polished arrow; in his quiver he hid me away." However, this verse does not make any explicit mention

---

7. Adelman, "Expulsion of Ishmael," para. 6.

of hunting. Instead, it seems to be describing personified Israel (49:3) as a weapon of God. Thus, Isa 49:2 metaphorically describes personalized Israel's (49:3) mouth as like a sword and the nation as an arrow tucked in God's quiver, ready to be fired. With multiple weapons mentioned, Isa 49:2–3 seems to be about Israel being a war machine, not hunting animals.

Like hunting, the trapping of animals is viewed negatively in the Bible. Birds were trapped and then used for sacrificial offerings to God and food.[8] Jeremiah 5:26 compares wicked men to fowlers (bird hunters/trappers). Hosea 9:8 GNT similarly parallels the enemies of God's prophet to bird trappers. Regarding enemy attacks on Israel (Ps 124:1–6), Ps 124:7 states, "We have escaped like a bird from the snare of the fowlers; the snare is broken, and we have escaped!" Psalm 91:3 states about God (91:2), "For he will deliver you from the snare of the fowler and from the deadly pestilence." Additionally, in Ps 141:9–10, David prays to God (141:8), "Keep me from the trap that they have laid for me and from the snares of evildoers! Let the wicked fall into their own nets, while I pass by safely." Regarding debt management (Prov 6:1–4 GNT), Prov 6:5 criticizes both hunters and fowlers, stating, "Save yourself like a gazelle from the hand of the hunter, like a bird from the hand of the fowler." Proverbs 7:22–23 CEV metaphorically compares a man committing adultery (7:18 CEV) with an unfaithful wife (7:9 CEV) to the experience of animals. Proverbs 7:22–23 CEV states, "At once he followed her like an ox on the way to be slaughtered, or like a fool on the way to be punished and killed with arrows. He was no more than a bird rushing into a trap, without knowing it would cost him his life."

The calloused recreation of fishing is also criticized in Scripture. Jeremiah 16:16 CEV associates fishing and hunting with enemies, recording God (16:15 CEV) as stating, "But for now, I am sending enemies who will catch you like fish and hunt you down like wild animals in the hills and the caves." Similarly, Hab 1:14–17 CEV compares the adversarial Babylonians (1:12 CEV) to fishers. The passage states, "The people you put on this earth are like fish or reptiles without a leader. Then an enemy comes along and takes them captive with hooks and nets. It makes him so happy that he offers sacrifices to his fishing nets, because they make him rich and provide choice foods. Will he keep hauling in his nets and destroying nations without showing mercy?" Fishing seems to be associated with destruction. In Ezek 26:3–6 NLT, God promises to help destroy the city of Tyre, stating that it will become a place where nets can be spread by fishers. Fishing

---

8. Hartford, "Traps and Snares," para. 3.

is often used as a metaphor for human punishment. For instance, Amos 4:1–3 GNT criticizes privileged and intemperate oppressive women who will be dragged away like fish that have been caught on hooks. Ezekiel 29:4 CEV describes God threatening pharaoh (29:1–3 CEV), stating, "I will put a hook in your jaw and pull you out of the water, and all the fish in your river will stick to your scaly body." Ezekiel 32:1–4 NLT also describes God threatening pharaoh, describing the Egyptian king as a sea monster who will be caught in God's net. God will then lethally abandon the ruler on land and let the wild animals feed on his corpse. Ezekiel 38:1–4 CEV similarly describes God threatening an evil ruler with a hook in the jaw. Then, the ruler and his military will be dragged away. These descriptions compel the reader to put themselves in the place of the caught fish. Would humans want to experience the treatment fish are subjected to (Matt 7:12; Luke 6:31)? The reader can further see what fish go through based on Job 41:1–34, which describes the great sea monster known as Leviathan.

For instance, Job 41:1–4 CEV states, "Can you catch a sea monster by using a fishhook? Can you tie its mouth shut with a rope? Can it be led around by a ring in its nose or a hook in its jaw? Will it beg for mercy? Will it surrender as a slave for life?" Job 41:5 CEV asks if Leviathan can be domesticated. Finally, Job 41:6–7 CEV then gruesomely states, "Is it ever chopped up and its pieces bargained for in the fish-market? Can it be killed with harpoons or spears?" Some verses are quite comprehensive in how they criticize killing animals. For example, Eccl 9:12 CEV castigates fishing and bird trapping, stating, "None of us know when we might fall victim to a sudden disaster and find ourselves like fish in a net or birds in a trap." Similarly, Eccl 7:26 likens an ungodly woman's heart to nets and snares. In conclusion, hunting, trapping, and fishing are viewed negatively throughout the Bible. Regarding fishing, I think that this biblical rebuke may partially be why Jesus led his disciples away from being fishermen, turning them instead into "fishers of men" (Luke 5:1–11). As the reader can see, many of the verses or passages in the Bible about hunting, trapping, and fishing should be considered "descriptive." None of these brutal activities are called "very good," like the peaceful vegan dominion (Gen 1:20–31) seen in the garden of Eden (2:15). Thus, veganism (1:29–31) should be seen as prescriptive—not commanded but certainly encouraged.

9

Questions about Interpretation

Why Did God Think Animal Sacrifices Were Pleasing?

CHRISTIANS SOMETIMES JUSTIFY ATROCITIES against animals with the belief that God was pleased by the sacrifices. This belief derives from the numerous verses which indicate that God was pleased with the animal sacrifices' aroma (Gen 8:20–21 NLT; Exod 29:15–25 CEV; Lev 1:1–17, 4:27–31, 8:18–28, 23:12–13, 18; Num 15:1–26, 28:1–31, 29:1–38). Christians may liken these verses to God enjoying the smell of a barbecue. However, it is not the scent itself that was significant to God, but rather what the smell represented. The aroma represented substitutionary atonement for transgression.[1] Thus, God was pleased with the aroma that represented substitutionary atonement. Romans 6:23 emphasizes the seriousness of sin, declaring that death is the cost of sin. Thus, the human who sinned was required to die. Instead, an unblemished (flawless) animal was sacrificed and considered an acceptable and theoretically equal substitution. The animal took the penalty that was deserved for the human's transgression. Thus, the human was temporarily (Heb 10:4) forgiven their sin (Lev 4:27–35 GNT). Therefore, animal sacrifice (bloodshedding) was required to temporarily (Heb 10:11 NLT) forgive human sin (9:22). Regardless, God permanently forgave all sin (10:16–18) because he is satisfied (1 John 4:10 CEV) and similarly pleased with the aroma of Jesus' sacrifice (Eph 5:2 NLT). Jesus was sacrificed in place of ungodly sinners (Rom 5:6–8). Notably, like the

---

1. Houdmann, "Why Would the Aroma," para. 2.

sacrificed animals, Jesus was also unblemished and flawless (1 Pet 1:19 GNT). The pleasing of God with the aroma of sacrifice shows equality between humans and animals. Importantly, the offering of Jesus ended animal sacrifice forever (Heb 10:12–18), as prophesied (Dan 9:26–27 GNT).

Why Was a Godly Man Like Samson So Cruel to Animals?

Samson was blessed by God (Judg 13:24) and was a man of faith (Heb 11:32–34). However, his behavior was often not indicative of this. Samson was a Nazirite (Judg 13:4–7), which required following a set of rules (Num 6:1–21) to separate oneself to God (6:2). One instance where it could be interpreted that Samson was cruel was when he tore apart a lion with his bare hands (Judg 14:5–6). However, Samson's lion-killing seems out of self-defense, which is biblically acceptable. For instance, David defended himself—and his father's goats and sheep—from wild animals like bears and lions, killing the vicious creatures if necessary (1 Sam 17:34–37 NLT). Lions and bears seem to have been a significant threat to human well-being in biblical times (Hos 5:14 CEV, 13:7–9), unlike today for the vast majority of humanity. Later, Samson scooped honey from the lion's corpse and ate some, and then later gave some of that honey to his parents, who ate some too (Judg 14:8–9). Samson broke one of the Nazirite rules by touching the lion's carcass. This one rule specifies not to get close to a corpse (Num 6:6). Later, Samson gifted a young goat to his wife (Judg 15:1 NLT), which seemed to have been customary (Gen 38:15–17 NLT). The goat, if female, was probably for milk (Prov 27:27) and, regardless of sex, eventually meat (Judg 6:19).

Most disturbingly, Samson rounded up three hundred foxes, bound their tails jointly in pairs, and attached a torch to every pair. He then ignited the torches and let the flame-carrying foxes invade the Philistine crop fields, ultimately destroying an ample amount of their produce (15:3–5 NLT). Rounding up foxes, fastening a torch to their tied tails, and letting them run would, without a doubt, qualify as animal cruelty (Prov 12:10 NLT). Samson's brutality probably led to three hundred foxes being burned alive. Additionally, Samson used a dead donkey's jawbone to kill one thousand Philistine men (Judg 15:15–17 NLT). Samson was far from ethical, which can be seen by his thirst for revenge. For instance, using torch ignited foxtails, Samson set fire to and destroyed much of the Philistine crops (15:3–5 NLT) out of revenge (15:11 NLT). Additionally, out of revenge

(16:28 NLT) for blinding him (16:20–21), Samson later killed (himself and) numerous Philistines (16:23–31). Yet, revenge is condemned in Prov 20:22. Samson was an example of a far from ethical person God worked through to achieve his will. God worked through Samson to confront the Philistines (Judg 14:1–4). Regardless, Samson's callousness towards the suffering of animals further indicates his lack of ethics. In conclusion, Samson's behavior towards animals should be seen as biblically descriptive, not prescriptive. Thus, Christians should not look to Samson as a guide on how to behave towards animals.

Does Dominion Mean "to Subdue" in Gen 1:26–28?

I have encountered animal oppressing Christians who try to make dominion mean something entirely contrary to the context. Just as a refresher, Gen 1:26–28 depicts God stating that humans have dominion over the animals. Dominion cannot mean humans can do anything they desire to animals because Gen 1:29–30 describes God telling humans (and animals) only to consume vegetation. Psalm 72:8 also uses the word dominion, and the context (72:1–17) describes the character of a good king. Furthermore, Ps 72:1–17 prophecies Jesus and his ruling as king. How did Jesus express dominion? In *I Will Abolish the Bow*, I implied that New Earth Abolition (NEA) reflects a proper (human) dominion over animals. NEA involves humans treating animals with Jesus' principles of equality (Matt 7:12, 22:39) and service (Mark 9:35). NEA also involves humans promoting harmony between and with animals, as described in Eden (Gen 1:20—2:8) and on the new earth (Isa 11:6–9; 65:17–25). Thus, human dominion means benevolently and compassionately caring for the animals (Gen 1:26–28).[2]

However, some Christians have interpreted human dominion over animals (1:26–28) differently. For instance, some conflate human dominion to mean "subdue." Cambridge Dictionary defines subdue as "to bring a person or group under control by using force."[3] These Christians then seem to interpret human dominion to be synonymous with God-commanded violent oppression of animals. These Christians understandably conflate the meanings of "subdue" and "dominion" because Gen 1:28 states, "And God blessed them. And God said to them, 'Be fruitful and multiply and fill the earth and *subdue* it, and have *dominion* over the fish of the sea and

2. King, *I Will Abolish the Bow*, 17–23.
3. "Subdue."

over the birds of the heavens and over every living thing that moves on the earth.'" Those two words are conflated because of their closeness in the verse. When *carefully* reading this verse, it is obvious that the two words discuss separate topics. In Gen 1:27–28, God told humans to have dominion over the animals and subdue the earth. These are different descriptions. In Eden (2:8), God wanted humans to live harmoniously and serve (Mark 9:35) the animals (Gen 1:20–31). In contrast, God meant for humans to be forceful and bring the properties of the land under control (1:27–28), such as the terrain, flora, and bodies of water. My explanation matches the context, as later, God had Adam name many animals (2:19–20). Meanwhile, God put Adam to work in the garden of Eden (2:15).

Another possible reason that human dominion over animals (1:26–28) is interpreted to mean "subdue" is because of Ps 8:6–8. This latter passage states, "You have given him dominion over the works of your hands; you have put all things under his feet, all sheep and oxen, and also the beasts of the field, the birds of the heavens, and the fish of the sea, whatever passes along the paths of the seas." Psalm 8:6–8's description of dominion seems much harsher than the gentle human dominion commanded in Gen 1:26–28. For instance, the expression, "put all things under his feet" (Ps 8:6) phrased elsewhere suggests violence and defeating enemies (1 Kgs 5:3; Pss 18:37–38, 47:2–3 NLT, 110:1; Mal 4:3; Rom 16:20). Importantly, the Hebrew word translated to the English "dominion" in Ps 8:6 is "*tamšîlêhū.*" This term does not match the Hebrew words used in Gen 1:26 (*wayirdū*) and 1:28 (*ūradū*) that translate to dominion. Additionally, Ps 72:8 translates the similar Hebrew *wayêrad* to mean dominion. Thus, despite the similarities, I do not believe Ps 8:6–8 references Gen 1:26–28 (and Ps 72:8), a generous and compassionate dominion that humans were ordered to have over animals. Psalm 8:6–8 seems to be a different type of dominion.

Within 1 Cor 15:27 NIV, Paul and Sosthenes (1:1) cite Ps 8:6 to indicate Jesus' current dominion over everyone and everything (except God the Father). Fittingly in Eph 1:21–22, Paul (1:1) states about Jesus (1:20), "Far above all rule and authority and power and dominion, and above every name that is named, not only in this age but also in the one to come. And he put all things under his feet and gave him as head over all things to the church." Jesus declares this dominion in Matt 28:18, stating to his disciples (28:16), "All authority in heaven and on earth has been given to me." Psalm 8:4–5 states, "What is man that you are mindful of him, and the son of man that you care for him? Yet you have made him a little lower than the heavenly beings and crowned him with glory and honor." Psalm 8:4–6 is paraphrased within Heb 2:6–8. Hebrews 2:5 assigns Heb 2:6–8 (and thus Ps 8:4–6) to the "world to come," also known as the eternal new earth (Isa 65:17–18).

Therefore, Ps 8:4–8 (and thus Heb 2:5–8) prophesies humanity regaining dominion over animals on the new earth (Rev 21:1). Second Timothy 2:10–12 and Rev 5:9–10 indicate that followers of Christ will rule the world to come. Therefore, Jesus will share his ruling dominion with his followers on the new earth (Matt 19:28). What does human dominion over animals (Ps 8:4–8) look like on the new earth (Rev 21:1)? Isaiah 11:6 CEV answers this question perfectly, stating, "Leopards will lie down with young goats, and wolves will rest with lambs. Calves and lions will eat together and be cared for by little children." Yet, why is new earth (Heb 2:5) human dominion over animals implied to be so harsh ("you have put all things under his feet") in Ps 8:4–8? This completed peaceful dominion will require the defeat of hostility. In the world to come (Heb 2:5–8), *the present violent nature of animals* will ultimately be defeated (Ps 8:4–8). Humans will then live peacefully with the animals, and all will be harmless (Isa 11:6–9 HCSB) on the eternal new earth (65:17–18).

Does God Want Animals to Serve Humans?

In *I Will Abolish the Bow*, I implied that Ps 72:1–17 is the model of how human dominion should be shown over animals (Gen 1:26–28), as "dominion" is used in Ps 72:8. Psalm 72:1–17 teaches that a king should be benevolent over the public. Likewise, humans as kings should be benevolent over animals (Gen 1:26–28). Psalm 72:1–17 is prophetic of Christ as King (Rev 17:14). Jesus taught equal reciprocity (Matt 7:12, 22:39) and servanthood (Mark 9:35). New Earth Abolition (NEA) can help guide human dominion over animals (Gen 1:26–28). I taught that New Earth Abolition (NEA) principles include humans treating animals how they would want to be treated and humans serving animals. The last principle of NEA is fostering the peaceful harmony between species (especially between humans and animals) seen in Eden (1:20—2:8) and on the new earth (Isa 11:6–9, 65:17–25; Hos 2:18 NIV).[4] One possible rebuttal to NEA is that the Bible could be interpreted differently. The Bible could instead be interpreted to mean that animals are supposed to serve humans, not humans are to serve animals.

4. King, *I Will Abolish the Bow*, 17–23.

For instance, Ps 72:11 states, "May all kings fall down before him, all nations serve him!" This verse means that the public should serve the king (72:1). Dominion (72:8) could then be interpreted that the public (72:11) serves the king (72:1). Human dominion over animals in Gen 1:26–28 could analogously be interpreted that animals (the public) should serve humans (the kings). This interpretation would cancel out the humans serving animals (Mark 9:35) component of NEA. However, an important traditional understanding of the Bible is that the New Testament interprets the Old Testament. Psalm 72:1–17 envisioned a righteous king that the public would serve (72:11). Though Jesus became Ps 72:1–17's righteous (1 Cor 1:30) King (Rev 17:14), Christ switched around the expectations of Ps 72:11. For instance, Jesus stated in Mark 10:45, "For even the Son of Man came not to be served *but to serve*, and to give his life as a ransom for many." Psalm 72:11 represents an expectation of a king (72:1) who would be served. However, Jesus switched the expectation, becoming the King (Matt 27:37) who serves instead (20:28). Likewise, humans should not expect to be served by animals. Rather, proper human dominion (Gen 1:26–28) would be to follow Christ's teaching and serve the animals (Luke 22:25–26 NLT). This expectation clarification sometimes happens in the Bible.

For instance, Ezek 40–48 in the OT prophesies a rebuilt brick-and-mortar temple, complete with animal sacrifices. Similarly, other OT verses like Isa 56:7 NLT and 60:7 NLT prophesy a physical temple where animal sacrifices will be reinstated. Additionally, Jer 33:18 in the OT prophecies animal sacrifices that will be reestablished and continue forever. However, in the NT, Jesus instead symbolically became (1 Cor 15:3–4) this temple (John 2:19–22; Rev 21:22).[5] Jesus specifically became the temple's foundation (1 Cor 3:11) and the cornerstone (Acts 4:11). The prophets and apostles are also part of the foundation. Believers are individual stones laid on the cornerstone and foundation to build a temple (Eph 2:20–22 NLT). This spiritual temple also includes believers, as symbolic priests, offering spiritual sacrifices (1 Pet 2:4–5 NLT)—like praise to God (Heb 13:15). God the Father's spirit dwells in this non-physical temple (Eph 2:20–22 NLT). God the Father (and Jesus) will be considered the temple (Rev 21:22) on the new earth (21:1). The OT prophesied a physical temple with physical animal sacrifices. However, the NT clarified that it would be a spiritual temple with spiritual sacrifices instead. The same principle applies for Ps 72:11. The OT sees dominion (72:8) as the public serving (72:11) the king

5. King, *I Will Abolish the Bow*, 73–74.

(72:1). In contrast, the NT clarifies that dominion (72:8) is instead the King (Rev 17:14) serving the public (Mark 10:45). Keeping with the metaphor— animals should not serve humans. Instead, to show true biblical dominion (Gen 1:26–28), humans, as good kings, should serve animals (Luke 22:25– 26 NLT). However, the NT also encourages believers (the public) to serve the King (John 19:1–3), Jesus (12:26; Col 3:23–24 NLT). Thus, analogously perhaps animals should serve humans, too. I will entertain the idea.

There is no evidence of animal exploitation in pre-fall Eden (Gen 1:1— 3:6). However, on the new earth (Rev 21:1), animals seem to be "exploited" by humans in some capacities, as evidenced by Isa 60:6 CSB and 66:20 NLT. Isaiah 60:6 CSB seems to describe camels transporting frankincense, gold, and possibly humans. Similarly, Isa 66:20 NLT describes humans riding mules, camels, and horses. Isaiah 66:20 NLT also indicates that wagons and chariots will be utilized to transport humans, which implies the use of animals. Wagons were commonly pulled by oxen (Num 7:3–8). Similarly, chariots were usually drawn by horses (Isa 43:17 NLT). I reasoned in *I Will Abolish the Bow* that the animals in Isa 66:20 could be symbolic of any form of human transportation (like trains), as animals were practically the only kind of land transport outside of walking when this was composed. I also reasoned that perhaps animals would be utilized for human transportation on the new earth (Rev 21:1). Although, importantly, it will be a world where animals and humans will no longer be able to be hurt or killed (21:4), which is not like the same beings on the current fallen earth (Gen 3:17–19). Riding animals as a hobby today does not precisely align with NEA; thus, our ministry advocates utilizing transportation that does not disturb animals in the meantime.[6] The same principles could apply to Isa 60:6 CSB. For instance, on the eternal new earth (65:17–18), humans may utilize any non-animal form of transportation (like cars) to transport objects. Thus, the camels in Isa 60:6 CSB could be symbolic. Regardless, if they are used for transporting things, the camels (60:6 CSB) could not be injured or killed on the new earth (Rev 21:1–4). This situation is unlike dromedaries here and now. Thus, humans exploiting animals for object transportation (Isa 60:6 CSB) does not align with NEA, as it does not serve the animals (Mark 9:35) or treat them as humans would want to be treated (Matt 7:12). Therefore, the Christian Animal Rights Association recommends using non-animal means to transport items until the new earth inaugurates (24:30). Regardless, suppose humans will utilize animals for transportation on the new

6. King, *I Will Abolish the Bow*, 100–101.

earth (2 Pet 3:13). In that case, it won't be morally problematic like it is now, possibly because of verbal consent.

Animals may be able to give verbal consent on the new earth (Isa 65:17). There is evidence that animals in heaven are able to speak (Rev 4:8–9, 5: 8–14, 8:13 DRB). Animals may have spoken before the fall (Gen 1:1—3:5). This claim is evidenced by the serpent speaking to Eve (3:1, 3:4–5), yet in her response (3:2–3), there is no evidence of surprise. Eve's (3:20) lack of surprise may indicate that animals routinely talked in the pre-fall garden of Eden (1:1—3:5). Although, the main refutation to this is that Satan was speaking through this serpent (Rev 12:9). Perhaps Satan was the one speaking, with the snake a mere vessel. However, an animal talked again after the fall (Gen 3:6). Balaam's donkey speaks to him after God seemingly made the donkey speak or, more likely, gave the donkey the ability to speak (Num 22:28–30). The donkey gives some personal details, so I think the donkey was given the ability to speak. Though it is slightly unclear, I infer that animals may be able to talk when the curse is removed (Rev 22:3 NLT) on the new earth (21:1)—just like (Ezek 36:35) the animals may have spoken in pre-fall Eden (Gen 1:1—3:5). Thus, consent could be obtained as to whether they would be alright with the transportation. Suppose animals can give verbal permission in the world to come (Luke 18:30 NLT). In that case, the idea of using animals for human transport (Isa 66:20 NLT) and transporting things (60:6 CSB) on the new earth (65:17) is not ethically troublesome. In fact, depending on the translation, Isa 60:6 (CSB, HCSB, ABPE, ISV, LSV, YLT) may indicate that camels will verbally praise God on the new earth (66:22). Maybe all animals will be able to speak then too?

Perhaps this is what Ps 72:11 meant when it interpreted what dominion meant in Ps 72:8—that the public should serve the king (72:1) *in benign forms*. I think Christ's teaching of kingly servanthood over the public (Luke 22:25–26 NLT) is proper dominion (Ps 72:8). Analogously, humans serving animals (Mark 9:35) is true dominion (Gen 1:26–28). However, with Ps 72:11 considered, maybe animals benignly serving humans may have also been the intention in Eden (Gen 2:8) when it was said humans have dominion over animals (1:26–28). Therefore, humans and animals would serve one another to glorify God and maintain the garden's well-being. Recall that the new earth (Isa 65:17) is a restoration (51:3) of Eden (Gen 2:8). In Eden (2:15), perhaps one form of benign service animals provided humans was transportation, as demonstrated by Isa 60:6 CSB and 66:20 NLT on the new earth (65:17). It could be interpreted that Isa 30:23–24 is about the new earth (65:17), meaning that one benign service animals could provide humans is working the ground. However, animals used for farm labor (Deut 22:10) may have come about after the fall (Gen 3:6), as only Adam was placed in the garden of Eden to keep and work it (2:15). Adam's equal (1:27) helper (2:18), the woman (2:22) later named Eve (3:20), probably helped him too. However, it could be interpreted that the animals were helpers, too, as the NKJV, CSB, HCSB, ABPE, and DRB translations of Gen 2:18–20 seem to suggest. Then Eve was created (2:21–23). Therefore, depending on translation, Gen 2:18–23 (NKJV, CSB, HCSB, ABPE, and DRB) could be interpreted as Eve being Adam's equal (1:27) helper, and the animals were also lesser helpers in Eden (2:8). This interpretation has good logical support, as many animals benefit the post-fall (3:6) ecosystem with their work. Therefore, perhaps the animals helped (2:18–20 CSB) the humans (2:7, 2:21–23 CSB) maintain the garden of Eden (2:15).

I theologically disagree, as other translations (NIV, NLT, ESV, BSB, NASB, GNT, NAB, NHEB, WEB) of Gen 2:18–20 seem to indicate that the animals were not suitable helpers at all. Thus, I interpret that in Eden (2:8), the animals' ideal existence involved resting, eating vegetation (1:30), and being taken care of (served) (Luke 22:25–26 NLT) by the humans (Gen 1:26–28). My interpretation of Eden (2:15) matches the utopian new earth (Isa 65:17) descriptions found in Isa 11:6–7 CEV. The passage states, "Leopards will lie down with young goats, and wolves will rest with lambs. Calves and lions will eat together and be cared for by little children. Cows and bears will share the same pasture; their young will rest side by side. Lions and oxen will both eat straw." Therefore, I interpret that only the humans (Gen 1:27) tended and worked the garden of Eden (2:15). I interpret animal exploitation for farm labor (Deut 22:10) as only occurring post-fall (Gen 3:6), probably because of the difficulty in growing edible plants from the cursed ground (3:17–23).[7] Thus, the use of animals for farm work (Deut 25:4) has a regulation pattern much like divorce.

Again, inseparable marriage is God's ideal (Gen 2:24), but God tolerates divorce because of humanity's hardness of heart (Matt 19:4–8). Thus, divorce is regulated (19:9).[8] Importantly, with Matt 19:1–12, Jesus implicitly encouraged believers to aspire toward the ideals of Eden (Gen 2:15–24). Similarly, Jesus implied that believers should work towards the ideals of the new earth (Matt 6:9–10). Likewise, ideally, animals should not be used to

7. King, *I Will Abolish the Bow*, 60.
8. King, *I Will Abolish the Bow*, 52–53.

work on farms, as reflected in Eden (Gen 1:1—3:5) and on the new earth (Rev 21:1). Because animal exploitation for farm labor is not ideal, it is regulated (Deut 25:4), like divorce (24:1). Christians should therefore work toward ending human use of animals in farm labor. Isaiah 30:23–24 could be interpreted as animals doing farm work on the curse-free (Rev 22:3 NLT) new earth (21:1), but I disagree. In *I Will Abolish the Bow*, I interpreted Isa 30:20–25 as taking place on the current cursed earth (Gen 3:17–23).[9] Notably, another farm animal work regulation in Deut 22:10 states, "You shall not plow with an ox and a donkey together." I believe that the Holy Spirit (John 14:26) is working toward eliminating the exploitation of animals in farm work with Isa 32:15–20.

Isaiah 32:9–14 prophesied a once populated city to be abandoned, and the fruit harvests would fail. Isaiah 32:15–18, 20 forecasts a restoration. Isaiah 32:15 prophesied that the Spirit from heaven would be given to believers. Accordingly, the Holy Spirit was sent from Jesus to the disciples (John 15:1 CEV) after Christ ascended (16:7 CEV) into heaven (Luke 24:50–51 CEV). Isaiah 32:15 also states that the wilderness will become a fruitful field and forest. Isaiah 32:16–18 then describes justice, righteousness, peace, quietness, and trust setting in forever. Additionally, the passage states Christians will live securely and rest in tranquil places. Isaiah 32:16–18 likely describes the eternal new earth (65:17–18). Isaiah 32:19 then seems to jump back to the adversity prophesied in Isa 32:9–14. Isaiah 32:19 appears very misplaced. However, Isa 32:9–20 might be prophetic foreshortening.[10] Thus, Isa 32:9–14 and 32:19 seem to take place on the current cursed earth (Gen 3:17–23). Meanwhile, Isa 32:15–18 and 32:20 seem to (mostly) be set on the eternal new earth (65:17–18). Although, scholars generally think that Isa 32:19 is a fragment that should be put directly after Isa 32:14 or that Isa 32:19 is an interpolation.[11] Interpolation is a text inserted later that is not authentic to the original manuscript. Regardless, Isa 32:20 then closes, stating, "Happy are you who sow beside all waters, who let the feet of the ox and the donkey range free." These are the same animals doing farm work (separately) in Deut 22:10, who in Isa 32:20 are no longer working the field because of the forest's fruitfulness (32:15). Importantly, in Isa 32:20 NLT, only the humans are doing farm work.

9. King, *I Will Abolish the Bow*, 99.

10. King, *I Will Abolish the Bow*, 90.

11. Dempsey and Butkus, *All Creation Is Groaning*.

I think that Isa 32:15–18, 20 was seeded with the arrival of the Holy Spirit (Pentecost in Acts 2:1–13). Isaiah 32:15–18, 20 will grow and grow in greater success until it reaches its final fulfillment on the new earth (65:17), where animals will no longer do farm work. It seems that on the new earth (65:17), animals will live in peace (65:25) and be taken care of by humans (11:6 CEV)—just like they were in Eden (Gen 1:20—2:8). Thus, the prophecy of Isa 32:15–18, 20 indicates that humans should be moving away from exploiting animals for farm labor here and now (Matt 6:10). Technology and mechanization (like tractors) have largely replaced farm animal labor in modernized countries. With this equipment, can humans let animals be free from farm work and thus (partly) fulfill Isa 32:15–18, 20 here and now (Matt 6:10)? Our ministry believes humanity can, with the help of the Holy Spirit (Rom 8:26–27). Therefore, in modern nations and where possible, the Christian Animal Rights Association advocates using non-animal means to do farm work. Sparing animals from doing farm work and using technology instead aligns with NEA, as it allows humans to serve animals (Mark 9:35) and treats them the way humans would want to be treated (Matt 7:12). Additionally, leaving animals out of farm work matches the harmony between humans and animals (Gen 1:20–31) seen in Eden (2:8). Only Adam was expected to keep and work the garden (2:15), with his wife helping him (2:18–25). Finally, leaving animals out of farm work matches the harmony between humans and animals seen on the new earth (Isa 11:6–9), where only the humans will do farm work (32:20 NLT).

Perhaps dominion in Ps 72:8 means that the public should serve (72:11) the king (72:1) in a benign form like companionship. Analogously, dominion in Gen 1:26–28 could mean that animals should serve humans in the form of companionship. Humans worldwide name companion animals, which indicates friendship. Human-animal friendship seemed to be the intention in Eden (1:20—2:8), as God desired Adam to name the animals, and Adam did (2:19–20).[12] This human-animal friendship will probably be carried over (Ezek 36:35) to the new earth (Isa 65:17), as humans and animals will have a close and harmonious relationship (11:6–9 CEV). Even on this fallen, cursed earth (Gen 3:17–19), the friendship between humans and animals is praised. For instance, in 2 Sam 12:1–15, Nathan convicts David of his sin by telling him a story about a poor man who purchased a tiny lamb. The poor man raised the lamb, who grew up amongst

---

12. King, *I Will Abolish the Bow*, 30.

his children. The lamb drank from his cup and rested in his arms. The poor man even considered the lamb to be like a daughter.

This lamb was obviously a companion to the impoverished man, just like dogs and cats under human care today. The story doesn't end well, as Nathan then tells of a wealthy man who owned countless livestock animals. Yet, the affluent man stole, killed, cooked, and served the poor man's companion lamb to a guest. David becomes enraged and says the wealthy man deserves to perish and must fourfold restore the lamb. The story (12:1–6) highlights the unfortunate property status of animals on this fallen, cursed earth (Gen 3:17–19), which I do not think existed in Eden (1:20—2:20) or will on the new earth (Isa 11:6-9).[13] More importantly, the story (2 Sam 12:1–6) praises human-animal companionship here and now, not just in Eden (Gen 1:20—2:20) and the new earth (Isa 11:6–9 CEV). Loyal friendship is praised in Prov 18:24 GNT. I think devoted friendship is the best service you can provide for someone. Thus, perhaps dominion in Ps 72:8 entails that the public should serve (72:11) the king (72:1) with loyal friendship (Prov 18:24 GNT). Analogously, I think the best type of service humans should expect from animals (Gen 1:26–28) is what that lamb gave to the poor man, companionship (2 Sam 12:1–3).

Why Does the Bible Tell Christians to Tread on Animals?

This question derives from Luke 10:19, which has Jesus stating, "Behold, I have given you authority to tread on serpents and scorpions, and over all the power of the enemy, and nothing shall hurt you." This verse could be read as Christians being authorized or commanded to harm animals. However, in context, this enemy is Satan (10:18), and these serpents and scorpions probably represent evil spirits (10:20 CEV). "Serpents" and "scorpions" are derogatory biblical terms. For instance, Matt 23:33 records Jesus calling the hypocritical Pharisees and scribes (23:29) "serpents." Additionally, Ezek 2:6 NIV calls the Israelite rebels against God (2:3–5 NIV) "scorpions." Regardless, in Luke 10:19, Jesus gave his seventy-two followers (10:1 CEV) control over demons in his name (10:17 CEV). Therefore, Luke 10:19 has seemingly little to do with animals.

Similarly, Ps 91:13 states, "You will tread on the lion and the adder; the young lion and the serpent you will trample underfoot." This verse also could be read as Christians being authorized or commanded to

---

13. King, *I Will Abolish the Bow*, 60–61.

harm animals. This verse also has connotations with Satan. For instance, 1 Pet 5:8 likens Satan to a roaring lion. Additionally, Satan is called the "ancient serpent" in Rev 12:9 and 20:2. These verses reference the Bible's beginning, as Satan is linked to the serpent who deceived Eve (Gen 3:1–6; 2 Cor 11:3). Christians are told to resist Satan (Eph 4:27, 6:11; Jas 4:7). Psalm 91:13 declares that Christians will tread and trample over Satan with the help of God (Rom 16:20), as prophesied (Gen 3:14–15). To tread (Ps 44:4–5) and trample (108:13 NIV) means to defeat. Psalm 91:13 could also partially be describing the hypocritical Pharisees and scribes (Matt 23:29), who are called "serpents" (23:33). Therefore, Ps 91:13 seemingly has little to do with animals.

Although, there is a literal fulfillment regarding the serpents in Luke 10:19 and possibly Ps 91:13. Acts 28:3–6 NLT describes Paul being bit by a poisonous snake yet not suffering from any harmful effects. Mark 16:17–18 NLT prophesied this interaction. Additionally, Ps 91:13 may find literal fulfillment on the new earth (Isa 65:17). Psalm 91:1–16 frequently shifts between time periods. For instance, Pss 91:5 and 91:10 seem to find fulfillment on the new earth (Rev 21:1), as that place is described as having no more night (22:5), war (Isa 2:4 CEV), evil (11:9 GNT), or plagues (Rev 21:4). However, Ps 91:11–12 seems to shift back to the fallen, cursed earth (Gen 3:17–19). Thus, Ps 91:13 may be referencing the new earth (Isa 65:17), where the *currently ferocious nature* of lions (2 Tim 4:17 CEV) and serpents (Isa 14:29 NLT) will be trodden (28:2–3) and trampled (25:10) under humanity's feet. In the world to come (Heb 2:5–8), *the present violent nature of animals* will ultimately be defeated (Ps 8:4–8). Instead, lions will be gentle, serpents will be harmless, and humans will live peacefully with the animals (Isa 11:6–9 HCSB) on the new earth (65:17).

The reader may be wondering why the biblical language around serpents, scorpions, and lions is so harsh. Hardly anyone in the modern world has to deal with the threat of wild animals. In biblical times, wild animals were a serious and potentially deadly threat (Jer 5:6). Those specific animals are no exception. For instance, the deadliness of serpents is described in Num 21:6 and Ps 140:3 GNT. The harmfulness of scorpions is portrayed in Rev 9:5 NIV and 9:10. Finally, the fierceness of lions is communicated in Job 10:16 and Hos 13:8. I am terrified of scorpions, so I understand the sentiment! I would not want to tangle with a snake or a lion either. Regardless, the next chapter is about questions pertaining specifically to the afterlife.

10

Questions about the Afterlife

Will Unclean Animals Exist on the New Earth?

SEVERAL VERSES COULD IMPLY that certain animals will not reside on the new earth (2 Pet 3:13) because of being considered "unclean." For instance, Rev 21:27 states, "But nothing unclean will ever enter it, nor anyone who does what is detestable or false, but only those who are written in the Lamb's book of life." If the kosher restrictions (Lev 11:1–47; Deut 14:1–21) are still applicable for Christians, Rev 21:27 could be read to mean that certain animals will not be present in the new Jerusalem (21:2), and therefore the new earth (21:1). Many species in Lev 11:1–47 and Deut 14:1–21 are declared unclean, which could exclude them from the hallowed town of new Jerusalem (Rev 21:2), and thus the new earth (21:1). However, this interpretation does not match Isa 11:6–9 CEV, which mentions several unclean animals on the new earth (65:17) like wolves, lions, leopards, bears (Lev 11:27), and snakes (11:30–31). However, the Greek word translated to "unclean" in Rev 21:27 is *koinon*, which means ceremonial uncleanness. In contrast, the Greek term meaning unclean animals is *akatharton*, which is not used in Rev 21:27. Although Rev 21:27 may be talking about moral uncleanliness, as the NLT translates *koinon* as "evil." Similarly, the HCSB, NHEB, and WEB translate *koinon* as "profane." For instance, Ezek 36:25 implies that idol worship can make one unclean. Idol worship is described as profane (20:39) and insinuated to be evil (1 Cor 10:14–21). Revelation 21:27 further states that those who do what is false or detestable will never enter the new Jerusalem (21:2). Therefore, I think Rev 21:27's statement of "nothing unclean" means sinful behavior will not be found in the holy city (21:2). This conclusion matches with Rev 21:8, which describes a list of humans who commit wrongdoing that will not be found in the new Jerusalem (21:2). That list (21:8), like Rev 21:27, also includes the word "detestable." Revelation 22:15 features a similar list of humans excluded from the holy city (21:2; 22:14) because of their sinful behavior.

Isaiah 52:1 similarly states, "Awake, awake, put on your strength, O Zion; put on your beautiful garments, O Jerusalem, the holy city; for there shall no more come into you the uncircumcised and the unclean." Isaiah 52:1, like Rev 21:27, could be read as many unclean animal species (Lev 11:1–47; Deut 14:1–21) being excluded from the new Jerusalem (Rev 21:2), and thus the new earth (21:1). However, in Isa 52:1, "and the unclean" is translated from the Hebrew waṭāmê. Elsewhere, waṭāmê (unclean) is solely associated with leprous disease (Lev 13:45). Therefore, Isa 52:1 seems to say that there will be no one with a contagious illness in the new Jerusalem (Rev 21:2). Isaiah 52:1 aligns with other passages which state that disease will no longer exist (35:5–6) on the new earth (66:22).

Finally, Isa 35:8–10 seemingly banishes unclean animals (Lev 11:1–47; Deut 14:1–21) from a sacred highway on the new earth (Isa 66:22). Isaiah 35:8 states, "And a highway shall be there, and it shall be called the Way of Holiness; the unclean shall not pass over it. It shall belong to those who walk on the way; even if they are fools, they shall not go astray." Isaiah 35:8 could be interpreted to be discussing unclean animals (Lev 11:1–47; Deut 14:1–21) because Isa 35:9 states, "No lion shall be there, nor shall any ravenous beast come up on it; they shall not be found there, but the redeemed shall walk there." Indeed, lions (Lev 11:27) and other ravenous beasts (11:1–47; Deut 14:1–21) are considered unclean, which could explain why they are not found on the holy highway (Isa 35:8–9). Additionally, Isa 35:8–10 could even be interpreted to mean that lions, (now) ravenous beasts, and other unclean animals (Lev 11:1–47; Deut 14:1–21) will be excluded from the new earth (Isa 66:22).

In rebuttal, Isa 35:8–10 could mean that lions (Lev 11:27), (now) ravenous beasts, and other unclean animals (11:1–47; Deut 14:1–21) will not be found on the holy highway but can be found elsewhere on the new earth (Isa 65:17–25). Although, I explained in *I Will Abolish the Bow* that Isa 35:9 is saying that the lion's current vicious and flesh-eating nature (Nah 2:11–13) will not be found on the new earth (Isa 65:17). Instead, peaceful straw-eating lions (11:6–7) will be present in the world to come (Mark 10:30

NLT). Thus, Isa 35:9 implies that lions (and all animals) will be nonviolent strict herbivores on the new earth (65:17–25).[1] Thus, I interpret that herbivorous and non-violent lions and beasts will be present on the new earth (66:22) Way of Holiness (35:8–10). Isaiah 35:9 may have another figurative meaning. Satan is likened to a prowling lion in 1 Pet 5:8. Similarly, Prov 28:15 compares a malevolent leader to a roaring lion. Likewise, Prov 20:2 CEV likens a furious potentate to a roaring lion. Additionally, Matt 7:15 equates false prophets with ravenous wolves. Therefore, Isa 35:8–10 figuratively could mean that on the new earth (66:22), there will be no angry malicious leaders (Dan 7:27) or false prophets (Zeph 3:13), nor will Satan be there (Rev 20:10). Importantly, is "the unclean" in Isa 35:8 even discussing animals?

Isaiah 35:8 may not be discussing unclean animals (Lev 11:1–47; Deut 14:1–21). In Isa 35:8, the English phrase "the unclean" is translated from the Hebrew ṭāmê, which is the same term used to specify unclean animals (Lev 11:4–5, 7; Deut 14:8, 10, 19) whose flesh is forbidden from eating and carcasses are commanded not to be touched (Lev 11:8; Deut 14:8). Although, the Hebrew ṭāmê (unclean) can also refer to a diseased human (Lev 13:46), a bodily discharge (15:2), bread (Ezek 4:13), offerings (Hag 2:14), and many other things. Importantly, animals are not "clean or unclean" in and of themselves, as evidenced by their creation (Gen 1:20–25, 2:19–20) in Eden (2:8). Animals were not distinguished as "clean or unclean" until after the fall (3:6–24), when sin and death came into the world (Rom 5:12 NLT). Animals were first distinguished as "clean or unclean" in Gen 7:2–3 NIV and 7:8–9 NIV for sacrifice (8:20). Although not explicit, the "clean or unclean" distinction was probably instituted for prior animal sacrifices (3:21, 4:1–7). "Clean or unclean" animal distinctions (7:2–3 NIV, 8–9 NIV; 8:20) were later extended to meat-eating (9:3–4)[2] and carcass touching (Lev 11:1–47; Deut 14:1–21).

However, Jesus' death (Mark 15:37) ended animal sacrifice forever (Heb 10:10–18 NLT), making the concept of "clean or unclean" animals (Gen 7:2–3 NIV, 8–9 NIV) null and void in the sacrificial sense (8:20). However, I believe the (secular) meat-eating and carcass touching meanings of "clean and unclean" (Lev 11:1–47; Deut 14:1–21) are still in effect on this current cursed earth (Gen 3:17–19). Notably, the new earth (Rev 21:1) will have no death (21:4). This lack of death (Isa 25:8) would make

1. King, *I Will Abolish the Bow*, 84–85.
2. "Distinction Between Clean and Unclean."

"clean or unclean" animals in the dietary and touching sense (Lev 11:1–47; Deut 14:1–21) null and void, as there will be no meat or carcasses, respectively. Thus, regarding Isa 35:8, 52:1, and Rev 21:27, there will be no such thing as a "clean or unclean" distinction (Lev 11:1–47; Deut 14:1–21) on the new earth (Isa 65:17) because animals will no longer die (11:6–9; 1 Cor 15:26). Therefore, the "unclean" mentioned in Isa 35:8, 52:1, and Rev 21:27 is not discussing animals. In conclusion, "clean or unclean" distinctions (Lev 11:1–47; Deut 14:1–21) will not have any relevance on the new earth (Isa 66:22) because humans will not be eating (11:6–9) or touching dead animals (25:8). One author put it this way: "Second, in the better world to come there will be no carnivores among men and animals. Hence there will be no need for the law making a distinction between clean and unclean animals insofar as diet is concerned, for men and animals will not devour one another then."[3] Although, this begs the question of what humans will eat on the new earth (65:17).

What Will Humans Eat on the New Earth?

Eating meat came after the fall (Gen 3:1–6). God allowed meat consumption (9:1–4) only after associating the human heart with evil intention (8:21). However, in Eden (2:15), humans (and animals) only ate vegetation (1:20–31)—a vegan diet. The new earth (Isa 65:17) is a restoration of Eden (51:3). No animals will be harmed or killed (65:25) in the world to come (Heb 2:5). Isaiah 11:9 GNT states that there will be nothing evil in the age to come (Luke 18:30). Therefore, all these indications imply that a vegan diet will be reinstated for humans and animals (Isa 11:6–9) on the eternal new earth (65:17–18). Thus, I think humans will eat various fruits (Rev 22:2), vegetables, nuts, seeds, and other plants. Animals, too, will only eat vegetation (Isa 11:7; 65:25). First Corinthians 6:13 is sometimes cited to show that humans will not eat on the new earth (2 Pet 3:13). In context, 1 Cor 6:13 discusses sexual immorality (6:18). First Corinthians 6:13 is thought to be about future new earth (Rev 21:1) bodies because 1 Cor 6:14 discusses believer (1:2) resurrection. However, 1 Cor 6:13 seems to be only talking about what happens to the stomach—and the food inside—at death. Notably, 1 Cor 15:42 says that the body is raised imperishable. Just like Jesus ate honeycomb or fish (Luke 24:41–43 NKJV) after his resurrection (24:2–6), resurrected (1 Cor 6:14) believers (1:2) in the future world

3. "Distinction Between Clean and Unclean," para. 6.

(Mark 10:30 NLT) would still theoretically require food. However, on the new earth (Rev 21:1), animals will not be harmed or killed (Isa 11:6–9), which would rule out meat.

Various translations of Isa 25:6 are sometimes cited to justify flesh-eating on the new earth (65:17). In *I Will Abolish the Bow*, I explained that Isa 25:6 is inaccurately translated to include meat. The typical word for meat (*bāśār*) is not present in the original Hebrew of Isa 25:6.[4] Based on Isa 25:7–8, Isa 25:6 may be discussing the new earth (Rev 21:1–4). Although the Hebrew is hard to clarify, I think Isa 25:6 GNT captures what the original language is trying to say the best. Isaiah 25:6 GNT states that there will be a banquet with the best wine and richest of food. Based on all indications, this rich food on the new earth (65:17) would be made of plant-based ingredients and exclude meat. Indeed, one author states about Isa 25:6–8, "When סמנים (rich foods) is used (this plural form occurs only here), one ought not think it refers to meat, but rather to foods that have been prepared using a lot of oil."[5] The new earth (65:17) is a return (Ezek 36:35) to Edenic conditions (Gen 1:20—2:8). Thus, Isa 25:6 GNT is likely implying food prepared with plentiful amounts of olive oil, as this fat is frequently mentioned elsewhere in the Bible (1 Kgs 17:12 CEV; Ezek 16:13 CEV). Therefore, all signals indicate that humans and animals will solely eat a vegan diet (Isa 11:6–9; 32:20 NLT) on the new earth (66:22). But will it be the whole new earth (65:17)?

Will New Earth Veganism Only Occur on the Holy Mountain?

I had one person criticize the idea that worldwide veganism will be reinstated (implied by Isa 11:6–9; 65:25) on the new earth (66:22). The critic stated that the implied veganism only describes what happens on the holy mountain of Isa 11:6–9 and 65:25. He meant that animals will still be exploited on the entire new earth (66:22) except on that one mountain (11:9; 65:25) and cited Isa 65:10 as evidence. First, to address the critic, the holy mountain of Isa 11:9 and 65:25 biblically means more than just a literal sacred summit. In the Bible, a mountain can often signify something beyond the obvious land elevation. For instance, mountains can symbolize difficulties (Matt 17:20, 21:21) or permanence (Ps 36:6). Importantly, a mountain

---

4. King, *I Will Abolish the Bow*, 82.

5. Foster, "'Feast of Wines,'" para. 15.

can symbolize a reigning government. For instance, by interpreting King Nebuchadnezzar's dream, Daniel prophesied that God's eternal kingdom would usurp all other earthly kingdoms (Dan 2:17–45).[6] In the dream (2:28), a large statue made of four different substances (2:31–33) gets struck by a stone and is destroyed. This stone developed into a large mountain and filled the entire earth (2:34–35). The idol of four different substances symbolizes four earthly kingdoms (2:36–43). Additionally, the stone represents God's kingdom, which would destroy all others and reign forever (2:44–45). Daniel 2:35 describes this stone which symbolizes God's eternal kingdom (2:44–45), stating, "But the stone that struck the image became a great mountain and filled the whole earth." Importantly, the stone became the holy mountain in Isa 11:6–9 and 65:25, which describes Edenic conditions (Gen 1:20—2:8) that will fill the whole earth—specifically the new earth (Isa 66:22). This makes sense, because Isa 11:9 implicitly prophecies the *whole* new earth (66:22) being filled with knowledge of God. Additionally, the holy mountain of Isa 11:6–9 and 65:25 represents God's final establishment of government as Isa 2:2 states, "It shall come to pass in the latter days that the mountain of the house of the LORD shall be established as the highest of the mountains, and shall be lifted up above the hills; and all the nations shall flow to it," as prophesied (Dan 2:44–45). The holy mountain (Isa 11:6–9; 65:25), and thus the entire new earth (66:22), will be filled with peace and serenity (2:2–4; Mic 4:1–5) for all species (Hos 2:18 NIV). Thus, no violence, harm, or death towards humans and animals (Isa 11:6–9) will occur on the new earth (66:22).

This same critic said that animals will not live peacefully on the new earth (66:22) because of Isa 65:10, which states, "Sharon shall become a pasture for flocks, and the Valley of Achor a place for herds to lie down, for my people who have sought me." The critic interpreted Isa 65:10 to mean that Christians (65:9) will harmfully exploit the flocks and herds on the new earth (66:22). Indeed, based on proximity, Isa 65:17 seems to link Isa 65:10 to the new earth. However, also in the vicinity is Isa 65:25, which implies that animals will not be harmed or killed. Isaiah 11:6–9 adds that humans and animals will not harm or kill on the new earth (66:22). Isaiah 65:10, then, cannot be about the animals being harmfully exploited. Isaiah 65:10 has to be read carefully to make sense. Isaiah 65:10 implies that on the new earth (65:17), herds will rest in the Valley of Achor and states that Sharon will develop into a pasture for flocks. What about the believing humans,

6. "Mount, Mountain," 444–46.

then? It will be the same way for them as the animals. Christians will also feed and rest comfortably on the new earth (66:22). I think the GWT interprets what Isa 65:10 is trying to say best. Isaiah 65:10 GWT implies that flocks will graze on the Sharon Plain pasture, and that cattle *and* Christians will rest in the Achor Valley. Therefore, Isa 65:10 matches the peaceful and harmonious relationship between animals and humans in other new earth (66:22) passages like Isa 11:6–9. Then to top it off, an earlier passage actually criticizes those who harmfully exploit animals on this presently cursed earth (Gen 3:17–19). There are rebels (Isa 65:2) who consume pig meat and have tainted meat broth in their bowls (65:4) who will be judged, repaid, and destroyed by God (65:6–8). Thus, we can be assured there will be no hurting or killing of animals for food on the new earth (65:17).

Why Does the Snake Still Eat Dust in Isaiah 65:25?

After Adam and Eve disobeyed (Gen 3:1–6), God pronounced a curse on the snake in Gen 3:14–15, stating, "Because you have done this, cursed are you above all livestock and above all beasts of the field; on your belly you shall go, and dust you shall eat all the days of your life. I will put enmity between you and the woman, and between your offspring and her offspring; he shall bruise your head, and you shall bruise his heel." However, we are told that nothing cursed (Rev 22:3) exists on the new earth (21:1). Yet, God states in Isa 65:25, "The wolf and the lamb shall graze together; the lion shall eat straw like the ox, *and dust shall be the serpent's food*. They shall not hurt or destroy in all my holy mountain." Importantly, how can Isa 65:25, which describes animals living in peace, be about the new earth (65:17) when the snakes are still cursed to eat dust? I have studied this in-depth and offer several different explanations:

1. The first possibility is that Isa 65:25 really takes place during the millennial kingdom (Rev 20:1–6). As a postmillennialist, I find that unlikely because I do not see how it is possible that humans could change the cursed nature of animals (Rom 8:20–22 CEV) so much that lions will only eat vegetation (Isa 65:25). Thus, realizing Isa 65:25 will require divine intervention—specifically the return of Jesus (Matt 16:27). A premillennialist would interpret Isa 65:25 as happening during the millennial reign of Christ (and his followers) (Rev 20:1–6), but

I disagree with that eschatology and interpretation. As a postmillennialist, I assign Isa 65:25 to the new earth (65:17).

2. The second possibility is that Isa 65:25 is to be understood as completely metaphorical. I find this explanation unlikely because God promises a restoration of Eden (51:3), and Isa 65:25 matches Eden (Gen 1:20—2:8). Therefore, Isa 65:25 should be understood primarily as literal.

3. The third possibility is that "*and dust shall be the serpent's food*" (65:25) was written to remind Christians that this is the new earth (65:17). This verse section could have been intended as a reminder that what the serpent did (Gen 3:1–6) in Eden (2:8) will not happen again. Since the serpent is (perhaps forever) cursed (3:14–15), a similar adverse event instigated by the snake (3:1–24) will not happen in the future world (Matt 12:32 NLT).[7] This possibility is problematic because Isa 65:17 GNT states that past events will not be remembered on the new earth.

4. The fourth possibility is that the serpent—and thus all snakes—has a perpetual (65:17–25) curse (Gen 3:14–15), and the rest of creation will have the curse (3:16–24) removed (Rev 22:3) on the new earth (21:1). This possibility would make sense as Gen 3:14 seems to indicate that the serpent—and thus all snakes—is cursed to eat dust forever. Perhaps the serpent's diet (Isa 65:25) is an exception to the rule in Rev 22:3. Sometimes there are exceptions. For instance, Jesus said there is no marriage on the new earth (Mark 12:25)—yet, there is a marriage between the church and Christ (Eph 5:31–32; Rev 19:7–9). Regardless, this possibility is problematic because snakes being forever punished by God (Gen 3:14–15) for the actions of Satan (Rev 20:2) seems unjust (Rom 9:14 GNT). Recall that before (Gen 3:1–6) the curse (3:14–15), Satan either possessed the snake or spoke through the serpent (Rev 12:9; 20:2).

5. The fifth possibility is that "*and dust shall be the serpent's food*" (Isa 65:25) is solely a metaphorical prophecy for the ultimate defeat of Satan (Rev 20:10). This possibility has merit because snakes do not seem to literally subsist on dust (Gen 3:14–15), and the phrase "eat dust" is a common idiom. For instance, the reader may have heard athletes that won with big margins say, "[The competition] ate my dust." This phrase means the athletes defeated the opposition. Similarly, Queen

7. Sharp, "Commentary on Isaiah 65:17–25," para. 10.

performed a song called "Another One Bites the Dust." I interpret the lyrics to be about failed romances. If somebody were to say that some- one "bit the dust," that would mean they were humiliatingly defeated. Micah 7:17 similarly uses this idiom, stating about humiliated nations (7:16), "They shall lick the dust like a serpent, like the crawling things of the earth; they shall come trembling out of their strongholds; they shall turn in dread to the LORD our God, and they shall be in fear of you." Similarly, Ps 72:9 states, "May desert tribes bow down before him, and his enemies lick the dust!" Perhaps the curse of "eating dust" (Gen 3:14) did not affect actual snakes but rather just Satan (Rev 12:9; 20:2), who masqueraded as a serpent (Gen 3:1–6). Thus, Satan was cursed to be humiliatingly defeated (Mic 7:16–17) throughout his life (Gen 3:14). Importantly, Gen 3:15 prophecies the final battle between Jesus and Satan (Rev 20:7–11). Therefore, Isa 65:25's statement about the serpent eating dust could be a metaphor prophesying the conclu- sive humiliating defeat (Mic 7:16–17) of Satan (Rev 20:10). Thus, the first part of Isa 65:25, "The wolf and the lamb shall graze together; the lion shall eat straw like the ox," as well as the third part, "They shall not hurt or destroy in all my holy mountain," are to be understood as a literal, as they line up with a restoration (Rev 22:1–5) of Eden (Gen 1:20—2:8). Thus, the second portion of Isa 65:25 (*"and dust shall be the serpent's food"*) prophetically symbolizes Satan's final humiliating defeat (Rev 20:10). The main problem with this possibility is that it would be disruptive and, to my knowledge, unprecedented for a verse to start literal, switch to metaphoric, and then go back to literal again. Additionally, specific details of Gen 3:14–15 align with the description of literal snakes much more than having anything to do with Satan (like the curse of slithering on their belly). Although, the serpent's (Sa- tan's) offspring in Gen 3:14–15 could be metaphorical for the Phari- sees and teachers of the law (Matt 23:29–33 GNT), or Satan's children (John 8:44 GNT; Acts 13:10; 1 John 3:10). Therefore, Isa 65:25 (*"and dust shall be the serpent's food"*) could be metaphorically prophesying Satan (Rev 20:10) and his offspring's (1 Cor 15:25–26 GNT) ultimate defeat. This possibility makes sense but I think Isa 65:25 is trying to communicate something literal too.

6. The sixth possibility is that the second part of Isa 65:25 (*"and dust shall be the serpent's food"*) does not correspond with the serpent (and his offspring) curse of Gen 3:14–15. The key is looking at the context of

Gen 3:14–15 and Isa 65:25. The difference is the type of dust and the surrounding descriptions. In Gen 3:14–15, God pronounces a curse, stating that the serpent (and his offspring) would be relegated to slither on his belly and *eat dust*. Genesis 3:17–19 is the key to understanding, as God states that *Adam is dust*, which corresponds with Gen 2:7 and 1 Cor 15:45–47. Ecclesiastes 3:19–20 expands on this idea, saying that all humans (1 Cor 15:48–49) and animals are (from the) dust. Thus, the serpent (and his offspring) being cursed to "eat dust" (Gen 3:14–15) means that snakes are now required to eat the bodies of other creatures (3:17–19; Eccl 3:19–20) to sustain themselves. The snake went from the blessing of eating vegetation in Eden (Gen 1:30—2:8) to being cursed to eat the bodies of other creatures, who are also now cursed to die (3:14–19; Eccl 3:19–20). Thus, part of the snake's (and his offspring's) curse is carnivory (Gen 3:14–19; Eccl 3:19–20). This claim becomes clear when one observes nature, as snakes are obligate carnivores and sometimes carrion scavengers on this cursed earth (Gen 3:17–19). Isaiah 65:25 then makes more sense with this context. The first part of Isa 65:25 describes wolves and lambs eating grass together and lions and oxen eating straw. Then the third part of Isa 65:25 implies that all animals will not harm or kill each other. Why, then, do the snakes still eat dust in Isa 65:25? Most importantly, Isa 65:25 takes place on the new earth (65:17), where death no longer exists (25:8) for all humans and animals (11:6–9). Thus, the snakes will still eat dust (65:25), but the dust will not be the contents of other beings as there will be no more curse (Rev 22:3) or death (21:4). Snakes will no longer be carnivorous, instead subsisting on (presumably) plant dust (Isa 65:25). This explanation fits much better with the context, as all the other animals will be strictly herbivorous on the new earth (65:17–25). Furthermore, these docile snakes in Isa 65:25 align with Isa 11:8–9 which describes children living peacefully with snakes on the new earth (65:17). This possibility is a good explanation, although a more straightforward reason could be best.

7. Finally, possibility seven is that there is no serpent curse (Gen 3:14–15) in Isa 65:25. Isaiah 65:25 says, "*And dust shall be the serpent's food.*" However, in Gen 3:14–15, God stated to the snake, "Because you have done this, cursed are you above all livestock and above all beasts of the field; on your belly you shall go, and dust you shall eat all the days of your life. I will put enmity between you and the woman, and between

your offspring and her offspring; he shall bruise your head, and you shall bruise his heel." The key is recognizing that the serpent (and his offspring) curse (3:14–15) has four parts and can only be complete with: (1) snakes slithering on their bellies, (2) snakes eating dust, (3) enmity between the woman and the serpent, and (4) hostility between further generations of humans and serpents. Isaiah 65:25 specifies that the snakes will eat dust. However, Isa 65:25 does not say that the serpents will slither on their bellies. An implication is that the snake had legs before his (and his offspring's) curse (Gen 3:14–15). Without specification, I think a reasonable assumption would be that snakes would regain their legs on the new earth (Isa 65:17). Isaiah 11:8 says snakes will reside in holes and dens in the ground on the new earth (65:17). This claim does not conflict with snakes having legs, as many legged animals live in holes in the ground now, like prairie dogs and ground squirrels. Likewise, many legged animals now live in underground dens, like rabbits and mice. The third part of the curse (enmity between the snake and the woman) (Gen 3:14–15) will be void. There is no indication that the hostile relationship between Eve and the snake (2 Cor 11:3) will be restored on the new earth (Rev 21:1). Additionally, the fourth part of the curse that specifies that there will be hostility between future generations of snakes and humans (Gen 3:14–15) will no longer exist on the new earth (2 Pet 3:13). For example, Isa 11:8–9 states, "The nursing child shall play over the hole of the cobra, and the weaned child shall put his hand on the adder's den. They shall not hurt or destroy in all my holy mountain; for the earth shall be full of the knowledge of the LORD as the waters cover the sea." Thus, on the new earth (Rev 21:1), the serpent and his offspring's four-part curse of Gen 3:14–15 will be broken. Only one of the stipulations (the snakes eating dust in Isa 65:25) will exist in the coming world (Heb 6:5 KJB). Without the other three parts (Gen 3:14–15), there is no curse present in Isa 65:25. Although, the reader may be wondering why the snakes would continue to eat dust (65:25) on the new earth (65:17). I theorize that perhaps the serpents are content with it, or Isa 65:25 is meant to convey that the snakes will no longer harm or kill anyone with their eating habits. It does not say that dust will be their *only* food. Maybe the dust will be a side dish! Similarly, I think that the wolves and lambs will not *just* eat grass, and the oxen and lions will not *only* eat straw. The animals in Isa 65:25, and thus all the animals on the new earth (65:17), will probably (51:3) eat a variety of green plants just like they were designed to in Eden (Gen 1:30—2:8). Although Gen 3:14-15 says that the serpent (and his offspring) will slither on his belly and eat dust every day of his life. However, this declaration could be referring to the snakes' lives on the current cursed earth (3:17-19), not their new magnificent lives (Rom 8:20-21 NLT) on the new earth (Isa 66:22).

In conclusion, I think Isa 65:25 ("*and dust shall be the serpent's food*") functions best as a dual interpretation. I believe that Isa 65:25 ("*and dust shall be the serpent's food*") signifies the ultimate defeat of Satan (Rev 20:10) and his offspring (1 Cor 15:25-26 GNT). Isaiah 65:25 also emphasizes that literal snakes will no longer harm or kill on the new earth (65:17). Therefore, I have concluded that on the new earth (66:22), snakes will live in peace with humans and animals (11:6-9) and not harm or kill anyone with their feeding (65:25).

What Is Meant by "a Little Child Shall Lead Them" in Isaiah 11:6?

The reader can see throughout this book that humanity has an extremely toxic relationship with animals. Because harming animals is such a normal part of life, Christians often find it hard to comprehend that there was once a time when humans showed peace to animals (Gen 1:20-31). Surprisingly, in my experience, Christians frequently struggle with the biblical prophecies that foretell a world of harmony between humans and animals (Isa 11:6-9; Hos 2:18 NIV). This struggle is especially evident regarding Isa 11:6. I have read Christian commentary that particularly emphasizes the description of a human child leading animals. Isaiah 11:6 is sometimes interpreted as a declaration of future human domination over animals. These believers seem to express pride, rejoicing that formerly fierce animals will be subjected to the power of even the most docile of humans. This unfortunate interpretation of human power is prideful and evidence that most believers have not accepted the role of a servant leader (Luke 22:25-26). Importantly, human servanthood is what is meant by the small child leading the animals in Isa 11:6. The Hebrew word *nōhēḡ* is translated to the English "shall lead" in Isa 11:6 and "you who lead" in Ps 80:1. Importantly, in Eccl 2:3, *nōhēḡ* is translated to "guiding." The context of Isa 11:6-7 includes formerly fierce animals resting, eating, and peacefully coexisting with tame, domesticated animals. Thus, the small child in Isa 11:6 is a servant, displaying a leadership (Luke 22:25–26) of gentle guidance to the animals and tending to them. I think Isa 11:6 CEV describes this beautiful future perfectly, stating, "Leopards will lie down with young goats, and wolves will rest with lambs. Calves and lions will eat together and be cared for by little children." Beyond the literal, the child in Isa 11:6 is also symbolic of all human believers (Matt 18:3). Therefore, a human job (Isa 11:6) on the new earth (65:17) will be to serve the animals (Luke 22:25–26).

Is Zechariah 2:4–5 about the New Earth?

Zechariah 2:4 NIV prophesies that Jerusalem will have no walls and will be filled with a large number of humans and animals. Zechariah 2:5 NIV indicates that God shall be a wall of fire around this future Jerusalem and the glory inside the city. Zechariah 2:4–5 seems to reference the new Jerusalem (Rev 21:2), a city on the new earth (21:1). Zechariah 2:4–5 aligns with several passages describing the new Jerusalem (Rev 21:2). For instance, the new Jerusalem (21:2) has the presence of humans (22:3–4) and God's glory (21:10–11). Additionally, the new earth (Isa 65:17) will include many species of animals (11:6–9; 65:25). It would only make sense that these new earth (66:22) animals populate the city of new Jerusalem (65:18). The obvious indication that Zech 2:4–5 NIV is not talking about the new Jerusalem (Rev 21:2) is that the passage says the city will have no walls. Yet Rev 21:12–21 says that the new Jerusalem (21:2) has walls. I think this can be reconciled by noting how large the new Jerusalem (21:2) will be. The new Jerusalem (21:2) will be approximately 1,380 miles in width, height, and length (21:16).[8] I interpret that Zech 2:4–5 NIV hyperbolically says there will be no walls around the city because the walls are so far apart. Similarly, Zech 2:5 NIV says God shall be a wall of flames around the future Jerusalem (2:4 NIV). Zechariah 2:5 NIV could be taken as literal because God's glory resembled a consuming fire at the peak of Mount Sinai (Exod 24:16–17). I think God "being a wall of flames" in Zech 2:5 NIV can also be interpreted figuratively because God is metaphorically described elsewhere using this phrase. For instance, Deut 4:24 states, "For the LORD your God is a consuming fire, a jealous God." Additionally, Heb 12:29 states, "for our God is a consuming fire." God is described as a devouring fire in Deut

8. King, *I Will Abolish the Bow*, 85.

9:1–3, signifying protection. Therefore, beyond the literal meaning, when Zech 2:4–5 NIV says that God will be a wall of flames around the city, this means that God will protect the new Jerusalem (Rev 21:2).

Additionally, the contexts of Zech 2:4–5 NIV and Rev 21:2 share many characteristics. For instance, Zech 2:1–2 NIV describes a man on his way to determine the length and width of Jerusalem using a measuring line. Similarly, Rev 21:15–16 NIV describes an angel who measured the new Jerusalem's (21:2) width, height, and length using a gold measuring rod. Is the guy with the measuring line (Zech 2:1–2 NIV) the same individual as the angel with a gold measuring rod (Rev 21:15–17 NIV)? I think so, because angels are often seen in the likeness of men (Judg 13:6–21; Luke 24:4–7; Acts 1:10–11). Thus, I reason that the man in Zech 2:1–2 NIV is also the angel in Rev 21:15–17 NIV. Likewise, I think the measuring line of Zech 2:1–2 NIV was generically describing the same gold measuring rod in Rev 21:15–17 NIV. Similarly, Zech 2:10–12 prophecies that in Jerusalem, God will live amongst Christians from numerous nations. Revelation 21:3 also prophecies that in the new Jerusalem (21:2), God will live among Christians. Revelation 22:2–5 likewise indicates that from the new Jerusalem (21:2), God the Father and Jesus will eternally reign with their believers from many countries. Although Zech 2:2, 2:4, and 2:12 state "Jerusalem," and Rev 21:2 says "new Jerusalem." These verses have no conflict as the OT frequently refers to the new Jerusalem (21:2) as just "Jerusalem" when discussing the eternal new earth city (Isa 65:17–18). Thus, depending on the context, the two town names describe the same place. In this instance, "Jerusalem" (Zech 2:2, 4, 12) is synonymous with "new Jerusalem" (Rev 21:2). Later, Rev 21:10 even calls the heavenly town just "Jerusalem." Taking these similarities into account, I deduce that Zech 2:4–5 prophecies many animals being present in new Jerusalem, the future holy city (Rev 21:2) on the new earth (21:1).

Certain translations of Zech 2:4, like the NLT, ESV, BSB, NKJV, AMP, HCSB, GNT, ISV, NHEB, and WEB, use the word "livestock," which is translated from the Hebrew "ûḇəhêmāh." This Hebrew word could be translated as "beast" (Ps 36:6), "cattle" (2 Chr 32:28), "livestock" (Jonah 4:11 NKJV), or "animal" (Neh 2:12) depending on the context. I think Zech 2:4–5 is a prophecy about the new Jerusalem (Rev 3:12) on the new earth (21:1). Therefore, since animals will not be property,[9] killed, or harmfully exploited (Isa 11:6–9) on the new earth (65:17), "livestock" would be an

---

9. King, *I Will Abolish the Bow*, 60–61.

inappropriate word choice for Zech 2:4. Appropriately, in Zech 2:4, the NIV, CSB, CEV, NET, and NRSV use the word "animals," which I think is the correct word choice. Therefore, I conclude that Zech 2:4–5 prophecies that the new Jerusalem, the holy city (Rev 21:2) on the new earth (21:1), will be populated by numerous animals and humans, and all will live peacefully without harm or death (Isa 11:6–9).

Epilogue

I HAVE LITTLE DOUBT that critics will read this book and stick to the same old excuses, clinging to texts like Luke 24:41–43 (where Jesus explicitly ate fish meat) to justify what they instinctively know is wrong. Regardless, with the new covenant of Hos 2:18 possibly starting after Pentecost (Acts 2:1), maybe Jesus meant to tell us that he ate the last piece of fish (Luke 24:41–43). Isaiah 25:8, although finding complete fulfillment on the eternal new earth (65:17–18), states, "*He will swallow up death forever*; and the Lord GOD will wipe away tears from all faces, and the reproach of his people he will take away from all the earth, for the LORD has spoken." For the already-vegan, I hope that this book has given you many rebuttals and talking points to utilize against the standard speciesist Christian rhetoric. For the uninitiated, I hope that this text has inspired you to be kind to animals and take up the cause of animal rights. I always tell the critics and the uninitiated: vegans are biblically morally correct (11:6–9), they are just a little too early (65:17–18)! For the critics, I hope that my book has inspired you to align yourself with God's ultimate plan of creating an eternal world free of crying, pain, and death (Rev 21:1–4).

Importantly, human pride is responsible for the greatest atrocity imaginable to our fellow earthlings. Human pride has not only negatively affected the animals, but also the environment and our health. If we humble ourselves, we humans can help heal our broken relationship with animals, the environment, and our own health. In principle, the Bible confirms this, as 2 Chr 7:14 states, "If my people who are called by my name humble themselves, and pray and seek my face and turn from their wicked ways, then I will hear from heaven and will forgive their sin and heal their land." We can help heal the land and its inhabitants by embracing the new covenant of Hos 2:18. I hope that my words can inspire Christians to humble themselves, which can lead to being kind to the creatures with whom we share the planet. This collective kindness will have a positive side-effect of recovering environmental and individual health.

Bibliography

Aaron. "Acts 10, Understanding Peter's Vision." *Path of Obedience* (blog), Feb 21, 2017. https://www.pathofobedience.com/scripture/acts/understanding-peters-vision/.

Adelman, Rachel. "The Expulsion of Ishmael: Who Is Being Tried?" 2016. https://www.thetorah.com/article/the-expulsion-of-ishmael-who-is-being-tried.

Alcorn, Randy. *Heaven*. Carol Stream, IL: Tyndale, 2004.

Bean, James. "Evidence That Jesus and the Original Aramaic Christians Were Vegetarians." *Sant Mat Meditation and Spirituality*, Mar 1, 2013. https://medium.com/sant-mat-meditation-and-spirituality/evidence-that-jesus-and-the-original-aramaic-christians-were-vegetarians-b8784ac42506.

Bignell, Scott. "John 21 Is Probably Not Original to the Gospel." *Jesus Tweezers* (blog), Jan 4, 2019. https://jesustweezers.home.blog/2019/01/04/john-21-is-probably-not-original-to-the-gospel/.

Burkitt, F. Crawford, ed. *Evangelion da-Mepharreshe Volume I: Text*. Cambridge: Cambridge University Press, 1904. https://ia800204.us.archive.org/22/items/cu31924092359680/cu31924092359680.pdf.

———, ed. *Evangelion da-Mepharreshe Volume II: Introduction and Notes*. Cambridge: Cambridge University Press, 1904. https://yeshua1blog.files.wordpress.com/2018/07/evangelion-da-mepharreshe-ii.pdf.

"But Didn't Jesus Eat Meat?" *SARX* (blog), Jan 22, 2021. https://sarx.org.uk/articles/christianity-and-animals/but-didnt-jesus-eat-meat/.

Christen, Caroline. "Meat Consumption in the U.S. Is Growing at an Alarming Rate." *Sentient Media*, Mar 17, 2021. https://sentientmedia.org/meat-consumption-in-the-us/.

Cisneros, Martin V. "Hosea 2:18: God's New Covenant between Man and Animal." All-Creatures, n.d. https://www.all-creatures.org/discuss/hosea2.18-mvc.html.

Cousens, Gabriel. *Conscious Eating*. Berkeley, CA: North Atlantic, 2000. https://books.google.com/books?id=lVUNFFnx6ZEC&printsec=frontcover#v=onepage&q&f=false.

Dempsey, Carol J., and Russell A. Butkus, eds. *All Creation Is Groaning: An Interdisciplinary Vision for Life in a Sacred Universe*. Collegeville, MN: Liturgical, 2015. https://books.google.com/books?id=wRJ9S4hbAoIC&printsec=frontcover#v=onepage&q&f=false.

"Desolate." Merriam-Webster, n.d. https://www.merriam-webster.com/dictionary/desolate.

"Did Jesus Eat Lamb?" *Swords to Plowshares* (blog), Feb 4, 2019. https://swords2plowshares.com/did-jesus-eat-lamb/.

"Did 'Jesus' Say Pigs Are Clean? A Study of Mark 7." *Truth Ignited Ministry* (blog), Nov 4, 2019. https://truthignitedministry.wordpress.com/did-jesus-say-pigs-are-clean-a-study-of-mark-7/.

"The Distinction Between Clean and Unclean Animals." *Ministry Magazine*, Jan, 1968. https://www.ministrymagazine.org/archive/1968/01/the-distinction-between-clean-and-unclean-animals.

"Do Fish Feel Pain? Not as Humans Do, Study Suggests." Forschungsverbund Berlin e.V. Translated by ScienceDaily, Aug 8, 2013. https://www.sciencedaily.com/releases/2013/08/130808123719.htm.

Duncan, Conrad. "Fish Can Feel Pain in Similar Way to Humans, Study Concludes." *The Independent*, Nov 22, 2019. https://www.independent.co.uk/news/science/fish-pain-human-animal-biology-lynne-sneddon-a9123626.html.

"Ebionites." New World Encyclopedia, n.d. https://www.newworldencyclopedia.org/entry/Ebionites.

Epiphanius. *The Panarion of Epiphanius of Salamis: Book I (Sects 1–46)*. 2nd ed. Translated by Frank Williams. Leiden, Netherlands: Brill, 2009. https://books.google.com/books?id=IKyxt9kyys8C&pg=PA150&lpg=PA150#v=onepage&q&f=false.

"The Facts." Cowspiracy: The Sustainability Secret, n.d. https://www.cowspiracy.com/facts.

"Famous Vegetarians (w/Short Quotes)." Christian Vegetarian Association, n.d. https://christianveg.org/famousveg.htm.

Fitzgerald, Amy J., et al. "Slaughterhouses and Increased Crime Rates: An Empirical Analysis of the Spillover From 'The Jungle' into the Surrounding Community." *Organization & Environment* 22.2 (Jun 2009) 158–84. https://doi.org/10.1177/1086026609338164.

"Foodprint—How Much Does Your Diet Contribute to Your Carbon Footprint?" *Oxygen House* (blog), Jan 4, 2019. https://www.oxygenhouse.com/blog/how-much-does-your-diet-contribute-to-your-carbon-footprint/.

Foster, Edgar. "'A Feast of Wines . . . of Fat Things Full of Marrow' (Isaiah 25:6)." *Foster's Theological Reflections* (blog), Oct 12, 2018. https://fosterheologicalreflections.blogspot.com/2018/10/a-feast-of-wines-of-fat-things-full-of.html.

Francis of Assisi. "God Requires That We Assist the Animals, When They Need Our Help. Each Being (Human or Creature) Has the Same Right of Protection." A-Z Quotes, n.d. https://www.azquotes.com/quote/848722.

Gentry, Kenneth L., Jr. "God's Divorce Decree in Revelation (8)." *Postmillennial Worldview* (blog), Mar 3, 2020. https://postmillennialworldview.com/2020/03/03/gods-divorce-decree-in-revelation-8/.

"George Carlin . . . It's Bad for Ya! Quotes." IMDb, https://www.imdb.com/title/tt0963207/quotes/?ref_=tt_trv_qu.

Gitamondoc, Ramon. "Answer to an Adventist on Romans 14." *The Splendor of the Church* (blog), Jul 24, 2020. https://thesplendorofthechurch.com/2020/07/24/answer-to-an-adventist-on-romans-14-by-prof-engr-ramon-gitamondoc/.

Gurney, Robert J. M. "The Carnivorous Nature and Suffering of Animals." *Journal of Creation* 18.3 (Dec 2004) 70–75. https://creation.com/the-carnivorous-nature-and-suffering-of-animals.

Hartford, Denny. "Traps and Snares." *Vital Signs Ministries* (blog), May, 2019. https://vitalsignsministries.org/newsletters/traps-and-snares/.

Hodge, Bodie, and Paul F. Taylor. "Doesn't the Bible Support Slavery?" *Answers in Genesis* (blog), Jan 19, 2015. https://answersingenesis.org/bible-questions/doesnt-the-bible-support-slavery/.

Hoffman, Frank L. "Luke 24:41–43." All-Creatures, n.d. https://www.all-creatures.org/discuss/svtluke24.41-43-flh.html.

Houdmann, S. Michael. "Old Covenant vs New Covenant—What Are the Differences?" *Got Questions Ministries* (blog), Apr 26, 2021. https://www.gotquestions.org/old-covenant-vs-new-covenant.html.

———. "Why Does God Desire Mercy and Acknowledgement of Him Instead of Sacrifice (Hosea 6:6)?" *Got Questions Ministries* (blog), Mar 7, 2022. https://www.gotquestions.org/mercy-not-sacrifice.html.

———. "Why Would the Aroma of a Sacrifice Be Important to God?" *Got Questions Ministries* (blog), Jan 4, 2022. https://www.gotquestions.org/aroma-sacrifice.html.

"How Would a Vegan Shift Help World Hunger & Decrease Food Waste?" Truth or Drought, n.d. https://www.truthordrought.com/food-waste-and-hunger#:~:text=Animal%20agriculture%20IS%20the%20ultimate.

"Hubris." Collins Dictionary, n.d. https://www.collinsdictionary.com/us/dictionary/english/hubris.

"Infidelity: It's a Right-Wing, Meat-Eaters' Thing." *NZ Herald*, Jan 25, 2012. https://www.nzherald.co.nz/lifestyle/infidelity-its-a-right-wing-meat-eaters-thing/NXPMFDR4FARB5L45NMFEIAXHKM/.

Judge, Maddie. "The Social and Ideological Foundations of Meat Consumption and Vegetarianism." *Faunalytics* (blog), Sep 25, 2012. https://faunalytics.org/the-social-and-ideological-foundations-of-meat-consumption-and-vegetarianism/.

Karlson, Henry. "Did the Post-Resurrection Jesus Eat Fish, and If He Did, What Does That Mean?" *A Little Bit of Nothing* (blog), Jun 10, 2019. https://www.patheos.com/blogs/henrykarlson/2019/06/did-the-post-resurrection-jesus-eat-fish-and-if-he-did-what-does-that-mean/.

Keener, Craig S. "Jesus Summons Us to Work toward God's Ideals (19:1–6)." In *Matthew*. IVP New Testament Commentary Series 1. https://www.biblegateway.com/resources/ivp-nt/Jesus-Summons-Us-Work-Toward-Gods-Ideals.

King, Matthew A. *I Will Abolish the Bow: Christianity, Personhood, and the End of Animal Exploitation*. Eugene, OR: Wipf & Stock, 2021.

———. *Meat: The New Cigarette: Patient Advocacy and the Plant-Based Diet*. Pennsauken, NJ: BookBaby, 2021.

———. "Organizational Theology." Christian Animal Rights Association. https://christiananimalrights.com/Organizational-Theology.

———. "Statement of Faith." Christian Animal Rights Association. https://christiananimalrights.com/Statement-of-Faith.

"Kingdom of God." New World Encyclopedia, n.d. https://www.newworldencyclopedia.org/entry/Kingdom_of_God.

Kinney, Will. "'And of an Honeycomb' (Luke 24:42)." The Insectman, Mar 26, 2016. https://www.insectman.us/articles/biblical/of-an-honeycomb.htm.

Kirby, Peter. "Acts of Thomas." Early Christian Writings, n.d. http://www.earlychristianwritings.com/actsthomas.html.

———. "Book of Acts of the Apostles." Early Christian Writings, n.d. http://www.earlychristianwritings.com/acts.html.

———. "The Book of Hebrews." Early Christian Writings, n.d. http://www. earlychristianwritings.com/hebrews.html.

———. "Gospel of the Ebionites." Early Christian Writings, n.d. http://www. earlychristianwritings.com/gospelebionites.html.

———. "Gospel of Luke." Early Christian Writings, n.d. http://www.earlychristianwritings. com/luke.html.

———. "Pseudo-Clementine Homilies." Early Christian Writings, n.d. http://www. earlychristianwritings.com/clementinehomilies.html.

———. "Pseudo-Clementine Recognitions." Early Christian Writings, n.d. http://www. earlychristianwritings.com/clementinerecognitions.html.

Koester, Helmut. *Introduction to the New Testament.* 2nd ed. Vol. 2 of 2. Berlin: De Gruyter, 2000. https://www.google.com/books/edition/Introduction_to_the_New_Testament/ thXUHM5udTcC?hl=en&gbpv=1&dq=Introduction+to+the+New+Testament+koest er&printsec=frontcover.

"Ktisma." Bible Study Tools, https://www.biblestudytools.com/lexicons/greek/nas/ktisma. html.

"Labor and Workers in the Food System." FoodPrint, Oct 8, 2018. https://foodprint.org/ issues/labor-workers-in-the-food-system/.

Link, Norbert. "Would You Please Explain Hebrews 13:9? Doesn't Paul Teach Here That We Are Free to Eat Whatever 'Meat' We Want?" Church of the Eternal God, Oct 22, 2010. https://www.eternalgod.org/q-a-9457/.

Lombrana, Laura Millan. "Climate Change Linked to 5 Million Deaths a Year, New Study Shows." *Bloomberg,* Jul 7, 2021. https://www.bloomberg.com/news/ articles/2021-07-07/climate-change-linked-to-5-million-deaths-a-year-new-study-shows?leadSource=uverify%20wall.

Loria, Joe. "What's a CAFO? Let Us Explain." *Mercy for Animals* (blog), Jun 5, 2017. https://mercyforanimals.org/blog/whats-a-cafo-let-us-explain/.

Miller, Dave. "Is Mark 16:9–20 Inspired?" *Reason and Revelation* 25.12 (Dec 2005) 89–96. https://apologeticspress.org/is-mark-169-20-inspired-704/.

Morris, Lindsay. "From E. Coli to COVID-19: How Animal Agriculture Spawns Infectious Diseases." *Forks over Knives* (blog), Apr 6, 2020. https://www.forksoverknives. com/wellness/coronavirus-e-coli-zoonotic-influenza-animal-agriculture-spawns-infectious-diseases/.

"Mount, Mountain." In *Insight on the Scriptures, Volume 2,* 1988, 443–46. Watchtower Online Library, 2022. https://wol.jw.org/en/wol/d/r1/lp-e/1200003125#h=1.

Newall, Marcello. "The Bible and Veganism: 14 Answers to 14 Objections." Shepherding All God's Creatures, Sep 2019. https://www.all-creatures.org/articles2/an-tpr-bible-veganism.pdf.

"Nimrod." Merriam-Webster, n.d. https://www.merriam-webster.com/dictionary/ Nimrod.

Papaioannou, Kim, and Michael Mxolisi Sokupa. "Does Colossians 2:16, 17 Abolish the Sabbath?" *Adventist Review,* Feb 22, 2012. https://adventistreview.org/2012-1506/2012-1506-14/.

Peter. "Is Being Vegan Healthy? Here's What the Top Nutritional Organizations Say." https://www.theplantway.com/is-vegan-healthy/.

"Pride." The Free Dictionary, n.d. https://www.thefreedictionary.com/pride.

Reckart, Timothy, dir. *The Star.* Culver City, CA: Sony Pictures Releasing, 2017.

Roat, Alyssa. "7 Facts You Didn't Know about Nimrod in the Bible." *Crosswalk* (blog), Dec 15, 2020. https://www.crosswalk.com/faith/bible-study/facts-about-nimrod-in-the-bible.html.

Sanders, Bas. "Global Animal Slaughter Statistics and Charts." *Faunalytics* (blog), Oct 10, 2018. https://faunalytics.org/global-animal-slaughter-statistics-and-charts/.

Schultz, Amy A., et al. "Residential Proximity to Concentrated Animal Feeding Operations and Allergic and Respiratory Disease." *Environment International* 130 (Sep 2019). https://doi.org/10.1016/j.envint.2019.104911.

Schwartz, Richard. "Jewish Dietary Laws (Kashrut): The Vegetarian Teachings of Rav Kook." https://www.jewishvirtuallibrary.org/the-vegetarian-teachings-of-rav-kook.

———. "Letters to the Editor." *The Jewish Press*, Jan 8, 2014. https://www.jewishpress.com/indepth/letters-to-the-editor/letters-to-the-editor-285/2014/01/08/3/.

Shafer-Elliott, Cynthia. "The Daily Stew? Everyday Meals in Ancient Israel." *ANE Today* 4.7 (Jul 2016). https://www.asor.org/anetoday/2016/07/the-daily-stew-everyday-meals-in-ancient-israel/.

Sharp, Carolyn J. "Commentary on Isaiah 65:17–25." *Working Preacher* (blog), Nov 17, 2019. https://www.workingpreacher.org/commentaries/revised-common-lectionary/ordinary-33-33/commentary-on-isaiah-6517-25-4.

"Slaughterhouse Workers." Food Empowerment Project, n.d. https://foodispower.org/human-labor-slavery/slaughterhouse-workers/.

Smith, Jamie. "What to Know about Vegan Diets." *Medical News Today*, Apr 27, 2020. https://www.medicalnewstoday.com/articles/149636.

Smith, Julie M. "The Ending of Mark's Gospel." *Brigham Young University New Testament Commentary* (blog), May 24, 2014. https://www.byunewtestamentcommentary.com/the-ending-of-marks-gospel/.

"Strangled." Bible Study Tools, https://www.biblestudytools.com/dictionary/strangled/.

"Subdue." Cambridge Dictionary, n.d. https://dictionary.cambridge.org/us/dictionary/english/subdue.

Tibbetts, James C. *Christian Insight into Biblical Nutrition Simplified*. Morrisville, NC: Lulu, 2018.

"Type 2 Diabetes and Vegan Diets." Vegan Health, n.d. https://veganhealth.org/chronic-disease-and-vegetarian-diets/type-2-diabetes-in-vegans/.

"Vegans Exploit Crop Workers." Acti-Veg, Feb 6, 2018. https://acti-veg.com/vegans-exploit-crop-workers/.

Walker, Larry. "The Surprise Sayings of Jesus Christ: Did Jesus Declare All Meats Clean?" *Beyond Today* (blog), Dec 10, 2002. https://www.ucg.org/good-news/the-surprise-sayings-of-jesus-christ-did-jesus-declare-all-meats-clean.

Wayne, Luke. "Are the Commands of Acts 15:20 Still Applicable Today?" *Christian Apologetics and Research Ministry* (blog), Jan 14, 2019. https://carm.org/about-bible-verses/are-the-commands-of-acts-1520-still-applicable-today/.

"What Would Jesus Eat? The Science within the Bible." *The Midlands Daily Online*, Mar 23, 2016. https://www.midlandscbd.com/articles/what-would-jesus-eat-the-science-within-the-bible-265.

Wheaton, Justin. "Did Yeshua Really Teach against the Dietary Laws in Mark 7? A Must-Read." *Who Is Like You Ministries* (blog), n.d. https://www.whoislikeyouministries.org/blog/did-yeshua-really-overturn-the-dietary-laws-in-mark-7-a-must-read.

"Why Are CAFOs Bad?" Sierra Club: Michigan Chapter, n.d. https://www.sierraclub.org/michigan/why-are-cafos-bad#sustainable.

BIBLIOGRAPHY

"Why Were Foods Offered to Idols Considered Unclean?" BibleAsk, Jun 25, 2020. https://bibleask.org/why-were-foods-offered-to-idols-considered-unclean/.

Zampa, Matthew. "99% of U.S. Farmed Animals Live on Factory Farms." *Sentient Media*, Apr 16, 2019. https://sentientmedia.org/u-s-farmed-animals-live-on-factory-farms/.

Zavada, Jack. "What Would Jesus Eat?" *Learn Religions* (blog), May 6, 2019. https://www.learnreligions.com/what-would-jesus-eat-700167.

Zucker, Jerry, dir. *Ghost*. Hollywood: Paramount Pictures, 1990.

Subject Index

Scripture Index

Proverbs

Ecclesiastes

www.ingramcontent.com/pod-product-compliance
Lightning Source LLC
Chambersburg PA
CBHW060342100426
42812CB00003B/1089